Praise for *The*

MW01625816

"I love this book! *The Relentle*
brokenness and God's love. Once I started reading, I couldn't stop. You will not believe what Scott went through to experience the goodness of God. I am reminded that my failures never scare God away. Scott's journey is raw, and God's love is apparent. This book will definitely grow your faith and encourage your life."

—Patrick Kelley, Senior/Founding Pastor, River Pointe Church

"Whew! That was a beautiful, hard, inspiring trip! Struggling with a ten-year addiction to crack cocaine, alternately fighting and then succumbing to it, Scott lost his successful business, his family - and his will to live. And then, in his darkest hour, God intervened, and Scott's life was forever changed. You owe it to yourself to be inspired by this beautiful, true story."

—Kent Whitaker, NYT Best Selling author of *Murder by Family*

"An incredible testimony of a continual struggle to find real life and happiness, and of God's love that won't quit. I loved reading Scott's story!"

—Kyle Moffitt, Senior Pastor, Normandy Christian Church

"Scott's true story is a powerful testimony of the evil selfishness of addiction that comes to kill, steal and destroy, and how Jesus gives us life, and life more abundantly. An amazing demonstration of God's grace and mercy, I highly recommend this book."

—Daniel Rice, Transformations/Prison Ministry, King's Cathedral

"After reading Scott's story, I see the power that addictions can have over an individual. It's also good to realize that we are never too far gone that God's love can't save us. I really appreciate the honesty in which the story is told, and wish I could have read a book like this when, as a former non-believer, I struggled with alcohol. A must read for anyone battling an addiction or just simply needing to be reminded of the greatness of God's love."

—Caesar Prelow, Pastor, New Hope International Church

"Scott's powerful and compelling story of personal loss and redemption will be encouraging to anyone, especially those who struggle with addiction. His life is a picture of how God is ready and able to redeem and restore our stories and set us free to write new chapters."

—Tanya Whitaker, Family Pastor, River Pointe Church

"Scott's story is a must read for anyone who has experienced a setback on the road to freedom from an addiction, and genuine encouragement for those who love them to keep on praying and believing God can still break through. Simply told with painful transparency, Scott takes us on his journey of repeated failure and loss. Yet, through it all, God's grace was in pursuit. A wonderful, faith-building, life-changing book!"

—Chaplain, Brigadier General Bobby V. Page, USAF (retired)

The Relentless Love of God

SAVED A WRETCH LIKE ME

Robert Scott Curran
with Anna D'Souza

ISBN 978-0-9980803-8-3 (Paperback Edition)

ISBN 978-0-9980803-9-0 (E-Book Edition)

Front cover design: Michael Cartwright

Printed in the United States of America

Published by Your Voice Creations
San Francisco, CA

This book is dedicated to my three wonderful sons:
Bryan, Kevin, and Sean

Contents

Foreword

"Scott, you know, your testimony is very powerful!"

Ann Gardner, who spoke these words to me, would know. She leads the prayer team at River Pointe Church in Richmond, Texas. They are the people who stand up front after each service, available to anyone who wishes to come up and be prayed for.

Earlier that week I had shared my testimony at an evening Bible Study that Ann hosted at her home. I had spent a month preparing my presentation, and it had been a humbling experience for me, baring my heart and sharing my faults with a group of people that I didn't know personally. I had talked non-stop for almost two hours. Well, actually, I did stop periodically; when sobbing while recounting my shameful behavior towards God, and when overwhelmed while reminiscing on His unfathomable love towards me.

The tears had flowed when I recounted how I had come to the realization that God was for real, and had been with me the whole time; that He had known first hand all that I had done, and had still loved me nonetheless.

One of my favorite sermons is titled 'Rahab,' from a series on 'Unsung Heroes' by Pastor Patrick Kelley at River Pointe. Rahab was a prostitute. Her story of coming to faith can be found in the book of Joshua in the Old Testament. She is mentioned several times as an example of God's great grace and mercy in the New Testament as well, including the eleventh chapter of the book of Hebrews (considered the Biblical Faith Hall of Fame). There you will find, along with many famous Patriarchs and Prophets like Abraham, Isaac, Jacob, and Moses - Rahab, the prostitute.

Pastor Kelley pointed out that Rahab never lost the 'prostitute' tag, as though God wants to remind the reader that no one, no matter what horrible choices they may have made, is beyond the long arm of the Lord.

The Apostle Paul, in a letter of exhortation to his young protégé Timothy, writes:

> *Here is a trustworthy saying that deserves full acceptance: Christ Jesus came into the world to save sinners – of whom I am the worst. But for that very reason I was shown mercy so that in me, the worst of sinners, Christ Jesus might display his immense patience as an example for those who would believe in him and receive eternal life.*
>
> - 1 Timothy 1:15-16 NIV

> *. . . God our Savior . . . wants all . . . to be saved and to come to a knowledge of the truth.*
>
> - 1 Timothy 2:3,4 NIV

The truth is that we are all sinners in need of a Savior. Jesus paid the price for our sins. God is for us, not against us. It is His desire that all be saved. Nothing good we do will cause Him to love us more and, better yet, nothing bad we do will cause Him to love us less. My prayer is that you will surrender your life to Jesus; ask Him to come into your heart and your life will never be the same.

I speak from personal experience.

Scott, the sinner

What good will it be for a man if
he gains the whole world,
yet forfeits his soul?

Matthew 16:26

Introduction

Life was good, from a worldly perspective. And that's the only view I had, having given up years ago on God wanting anything to do with me. I didn't even know if God actually existed. And I tried hard not to care.

I had gone from rags to riches, worked hard, really hard, and had a thriving business which put me in contact with Hollywood celebrities and the superstars of the Sports world. I owned a beautiful home on Maui and had also purchased a vacant lot with a partner in an exclusive gated community where the views were spectacular. The plan was to build a new house on that lot and retire.

If fate hadn't intervened, if I hadn't made a horrible choice one lonely night, I'd be living in that house right now. How sad that would be, living large but never having a relationship with Jesus. Fortunately, I ended up losing everything and gained something far greater than this world has to offer – my eternal salvation and a home prepared for me forever in heaven.

I can totally relate to the Apostle Paul's sentiments in his letter to the church in Philippi:

> *What is more, I consider everything a loss because of the surpassing worth of knowing Christ Jesus my Lord, for whose sake I have lost all things.*
>
> - Philippians 3:8 NIV

Allow me to paraphrase what David says in Psalm 40. In my darkest hour, God brought me up out of a horrible pit, out of the mud and miry clay, and set my feet upon a rock and established my steps. He put a new song in my mouth, a hymn of praise to our God.

Preface

I was raised Catholic and educated in Catholic schools through the ninth grade. In all those years we never ever read the Bible - not in school and not at home. It was a completely alien book to me. Instead, I was schooled in all the rituals and traditions of the religion and was taught that only Catholics could go to heaven.

The Mass is the primary ritual in Catholicism. It is a solemn ceremony in which the priest supposedly converts the tiny wafers of bread into the actual body of Jesus, and the wine into the actual blood of Jesus through a mysterious process known as Transubstantiation. Following this mystical transformation performed at the altar, the faithful then line up to reverently partake of Holy Communion.

As a child, the prospect of SIN filled me with much fear and trepidation; not so much the actual fact of it, but it's dire consequences. The Catholic religion divided sin into two categories; venial sins, which were minor offenses, and mortal sins which were major infractions. We were told that if we died with venial sins on our soul, we would go to a mysterious place called purgatory, where we would be punished for who knows how long. However, dying with a mortal sin on our soul would be a ticket straight to hell.

No wonder then that I lived in constant and morbid fear of sin, but, scared as I was of Purgatory, it was still a far better fate than that of my non-Catholic, heathen friends. They were all headed straight to hell just because they weren't Catholics.

But what if I suddenly died with a mortal sin on my soul? Wouldn't hell be my eternal destination as well?

Fortunately, there was a Catholic remedy for these concerns of mine as well. It was in the form of the Confessional, a box-like closet divided by a meshed screen through which the repentant sinner confessed his sins to a priest on the other side, with the assured promise of anonymity. After listening to all the sins committed since the last confession, the priest would then assign a suitable penance for the confessor, which usually included repeating several "Hail Marys" and "Our Fathers" on one's knees; the number of repetitions depending on the severity of the sins confessed.

I always tried my absolute best to remember and confess all my sins, conscious of the fact that the alternative to forgetting any would result in either purgatorial punishment or an eternity in Hell. I definitely didn't want to go to hell, and I certainly didn't want to rot in Purgatory either.

Then one day when I was twelve years old, I confessed a rather embarrassing personal sin to the priest, comforted by the fact that he wouldn't know who I was. After pronouncing the absolution, the priest assigned my penance: "Go and say 5 Hail Marys and 3 Our Fathers, Scott."

SCOTT! The priest knew who I was! He had known all along who was confessing that mortifying sin!

I was so embarrassed I never went to a confessional again. This meant that I could never take Communion at Mass and since the Eucharist was a strict Catholic requirement for salvation, I found myself caught in a tight doctrinal bind with seemingly no way out.

It was only a matter of time before I quit attending church altogether. I had been so heavily indoctrinated with the belief that only Catholics had any chance of going to heaven, switching to another religion was not even an option for me. I felt I had failed all of God's basic requirements, so what hope was left for my salvation? God was angry and disappointed with me - of that, I was convinced.

But God had other plans, plans that had nothing to do with following a religion and everything to do with establishing a relationship with Him.

If you had told me then that one day I would have an intimate relationship with Jesus, I would have scoffed at you. If you had said to me that I would be serving God and singing His praises to the world, I would have scorned your prophecy.

Yet here I am today, a lover of Jesus, and a servant of the King. It's been a long and arduous journey to get here, and God's relentless love was with me every step of the broken way.

This is my story.

1

Rebel Rising

I was born in the city of Spokane, Washington, in 1951. By the time I was fourteen years old we had moved to seven different towns throughout the State, and our family had grown to six kids. I was the oldest, my brother the youngest, and there were four sisters sandwiched in between.

Our constant relocating was creating a restlessness within me that wasn't helped by my father's cynical and negative disposition. Dad apparently wasn't convinced that affirmation was a healthy parenting technique, so I grew up feeling like I could do nothing good enough in his eyes. What hurt me more was that he rarely showed any loving affection toward my wonderful mom, and always seemed to be criticizing her.

It didn't help either that I held on to a simmering resentment for the way my dad physically punished me when I was a little kid. Without going into specifics, I'll just say it was over-the-top brutal, and I grew up disliking my dad intensely. My rebellious attitude soon morphed into complete disrespect toward all forms of authority - teachers, coaches, umpires, referees, bosses, police; all became recipients of my vented frustration.

During the Sixties, the seed of counterculture began germinating in society. Bastions of cultural traditions were tumbling down, as political and sexual revolutions were gaining momentum. It was a confusing and disruptive era to be growing up in.

Excelling in sports became an obsession for me as it was a place where my self-esteem could flourish. I graduated from High School in 1970 with some pretty good grades, but College made sure my grades died a natural death. Parties, girls, and basketball took precedence over my studies, and my decadent lifestyle resulted in me being transferred to three colleges in five years. I made the varsity basketball team at two of the colleges, quitting the first team, and breaking my foot and eventually getting suspended from the second. Without basketball, I developed a serious identity crisis and dropped out of school for good.

Or should I say for worse? By the fall of 1976, I was just another long-haired, pot-smoking, motorcycle-riding hippie living in a rundown duplex in cold, rainy North Seattle- with no money, no job, no steady girlfriend, and no clue about anything.

One thing I did know for sure - the miserable, depressing weather of Seattle, while it matched my disposition, wasn't going to improve until summer, and that was several months away. So I thought, what the heck, I might as well go somewhere sunny, bright and warm. I didn't know how I would survive, without knowing anyone, and with only a few dollars in my pocket, but I knew I needed to do something.

So I called up my best friend, Brad Hillard, to see if he could come up with the $400 I had loaned him a while back so I could purchase an airline ticket.

"Hey, Hillard, I was wondering if there is any way you could pay back the money I loaned you."

"Sure. How soon do you need it?"

"As soon as possible. I'm outta here."

"Where ya goin'?"

"Maui."

2

Maui

A week before Thanksgiving I walked off the plane at Kahului airport on Maui, carrying two duffle bags, and with $150 in cash and two $90 unemployment checks in my pockets. A three-day car rental gobbled up a quick $50 of my meager funds. When I asked the rental agent advice on where I should go, she suggested the historic whaling town of Lahaina and showed me on a map in a tourist brochure how to get there.

It was a beautiful sunny day, with cottony clouds ambling across the azure sky. Haleakala, a 10,000-foot dormant volcano, rose majestically on my left, and the stately West Maui Mountains on my right, as I drove across the island. The route soon hugged the coastline, the sun now glimmering off the crystal clear blue ocean, the Island of Lanai rising in the distance.

I turned off at Lahaina and drove down Front Street. On one side sailboats idled lazily just offshore, on the other touristy shops and bars beckoned. Surfer dudes were hanging out in swim shorts, suntanned girls were parading in bikini tops, and just about everyone was wearing flip-flops.

I said to myself, "Good call, Scott."

Suddenly, I noticed some friends I used to fool around with at my last college in Bellingham, Washington. While I was attending, loosely speaking, school there, they were building a magnificent 48' two-masted sailboat, named "Odle," on their rental property. What a surprise to find out they had sailed to Maui! Even better, they invited me to live with them on their sailboat. This was extremely fortunate, as I soon learned that finding a place to rent was nearly impossible; I didn't have rent money anyway. In fact, people were renting tent space on their yards for $300/month, which explained all the tents I saw surrounding the houses along Front Street.

Jobs, however, were plentiful, and within a couple of days, I got hired as a bookkeeper at the Maui Eldorado condominium in Kaanapali Resort, the major resort area on Maui in 1976. I snuck into the Employees' locker room at a nearby hotel, commandeered a locker to store my meager belongings, and happily used their showers.

Two months after my arrival, when my friends sailed off to Tahiti, I rented a small trailer in a wrecking yard for a month. After that, I slept on a fishing boat for several weeks. This was the worst. The fishing boat was anchored offshore, so every evening I would have to swim out to it then before daybreak swim back to shore. It was five months since arriving on the island before I was finally able to enjoy a semi-normal living situation, thanks to two lady friends I had known in Seattle who decided to fly out and join me. They rented a studio apartment at a sketchy place called

Honokowai East, which we called the Honokowai Least, and invited me to stay with them. None of us had a car, so we hitchhiked or rode bicycles to get around.

The new friendships I developed came mostly through playing basketball at the Lahaina Civic Center and playing in a softball league. Just about everyone seemed to be a pilgrim like myself, escaping various parts of the mainland in search of adventure and a better life. It was a bond we all shared, just learning to survive together on the island.

When summer rolled around I went back to Seattle, but after three months I realized my life there was a dead end and I returned to Maui. I couch surfed with friends at their two-bedroom apartment in Lahaina, and eventually, one of the rooms became available, and I moved into it. I began working weekends as a night auditor and also started my own window cleaning business - 'Tropical Window Cleaning.' I used what little money I had to purchase an old Ford Falcon with surf racks which were perfect for strapping on a ladder.

In 1979 I got married, and my wife and I rented a one-room guest cottage in Kihei. I was no longer night auditing but continued cleaning windows and also began working as a banquet waiter at two hotels. On top of all this I got my Real Estate license. I was becoming a workaholic.

In February of 1980 our son Sean was born, and later that year we bought a small home in Kihei. But our marriage didn't survive, and in 1983 my now ex-wife moved to Connecticut with her boyfriend and Sean.

My son was now 6,000 miles away. I was devastated.

3

Video Production

Work became an obsession. I signed on as a Banquet waiter at two more hotels. Most days I would work a breakfast function at one hotel, clean windows for several hours, and then go to another hotel to work a dinner function. If I had any free time, I would do research at the Real Estate office or sit an Open House. The only extended time I ever took off was two weeks in the summer to go on vacation at my family's cabin in Priest Lake, Idaho.

In 1986 I got married again, and in May the following year my son Kevin was born. It was during this time while waiting on tables at corporate banquets that I noticed a steady increase in video crews being flown in from the Mainland to produce videos of all the activities and parties; videos that would be shown to the groups at their final night awards ceremony and used as promotional advertising. Video was still in its infancy, photography and slideshows remained the norms, but I perceived an industry that would only grow rapidly popular. Although I didn't know anything about the video business, I did know I didn't want to be waiting tables and cleaning windows my whole life. Therefore, I thought this would be a good time to channel my entrepreneurial streak.

The first thing I had to decide was what equipment to purchase. As there was no internet in those days, I flew to Honolulu and met with the few people there that were in the video industry, visited the TV stations, read trade magazines, and called production companies on the mainland, bugging the heck out of them with all my questions. After several months of research, I finally plunked down my entire savings, $14,000, on a camera, tripod, and accessories.

I taught myself all the technical workings from the service manuals that came with the equipment and from the trade magazines in the mail. My favorite magazine, which I received monthly, was Video Systems. It contained all kinds of instruction on lighting, audio recording, shooting techniques and the like. The artistic side I learned from a book written in the 1950's entitled 'The 5C's of Cinematography,' which were: Camera angles, Composition, Close-ups, Continuity, and Cutting (editing). Along with written instructions, the book included lots of pictures and diagrams which made it all easily understandable. I would cross-reference what I learned from the book with what I would be watching on the television and vice versa. It was as simple as that!

So now it was time to market my services. I was smart enough not to put all my eggs in the video basket and was still working my other jobs – banquet waiter at four resorts, real estate sales, and window cleaning- so there was no financial pressure on me to succeed immediately. The best thing about these jobs was that I could dictate my own scheduling and stay flexible for whatever video gigs I could find.

I started out by shooting Youth soccer games, offering to videotape any games that the teams could guarantee me a minimum of 10 VHS sales at $20 each. I drew up flyers for the coaches to give to their players at practice, which the players then took home to their parents. Video was a novelty in those days, and as no one had their own video cameras, the response was very enthusiastic. I then made the same presentation to the Youth Football leagues. This turned out to be much more lucrative than soccer – more players, more tape sales. Even the parents of the cheerleaders ordered videos.

Weddings were next. At that time, there were only three wedding planners on Maui, and their clients were mostly tourists. What better way to share their wedding with friends and family back home than with a video? It was a little awkward working with the wedding photographers at first as they saw video as an intrusion in their own market, but they soon reluctantly accepted it as the norm. The tourist wedding industry became my bread and butter, and within a short period, I was shooting several weddings a week.

During this time I also contacted the ABC, CBS and NBC television stations based in Honolulu, and they began hiring me to shoot their News, Sports and Special Events on Maui. Eventually, these jobs got me connected to other networks, and before long I was doing work for CNN and ESPN as well.

As the income from my video business increased, I slowly began quitting my other jobs. The first to go was Real Estate – it could be really discouraging - but at least it had taught me follow-up, marketing, and sales techniques, skills that served me well in my new venture. Then I quit the banquet waiter jobs, one at a time, as the continued uptick in video income equaled the money I was making at each of the four hotels. I did continue to clean windows, and I also got a job selling TV advertising with the local Cablevision Company.

One day a photographer friend asked me what it would cost to shoot a PSA (Public Service Announcement) and if I could get it included in Cablevision's programming. He told me that a building at Teen Challenge had been entirely destroyed in a fire and they needed funds to restore it. I said I'd be happy to shoot it for free and would get it on the air. A couple of weeks later, my friend told me that a tourist staying at the Marriott Hotel, after seeing the Teen Challenge PSA on Cable, had sent in a check for $10,000. Hearing that made me feel really good.

The reason I had started the Video Production business in the first place was to produce corporate convention videos, and I finally got my first convention gig by giving an Event Planner my business card while I was waiting tables at an event for Sony Corporation. She asked if I could produce a video for their next group which was arriving in just a few days. I eagerly said yes, thinking to myself 'Oh my, what I had been hoping for is now actually going to happen!'

The project consisted of four days of shooting all their activities, parties and events. When I wasn't shooting, I was editing - incorporating music, sound effects, funny skits, and stock footage of Maui and the resort where they were staying. On the final night of their convention, I was sitting backstage as the audiovisual company played my video during their awards banquet. As the video ended the ballroom erupted into applause, a flood of emotions welled up inside of me, and I broke down and cried.

Soon after that, an employee I worked with at Cablevision talked me into going into partnership with him. He had extensive experience working for a major television network, so I thought this would work out great. We leased $50,000 worth of equipment, got rolling, and then he suddenly decided to dissolve the partnership. I had been duped. To add insult to injury, my manager at Cablevision used the friction between my former partner and myself as an excuse to fire me. This allowed her to grab all of my clients and the continuous monthly advertising revenue that I had worked so hard to generate.

It was during this stressful time that my marriage to Kevin's mom began to unravel as well. We decided to sell our house, and I rented a two-bedroom condo to live in. She eventually met someone else, remarried and moved into a beautiful home in Wailea. I was thankful that I would at least be able to see Kevin on a regular basis.

In the summers I would fly Sean out from Connecticut, and then take him and Kevin with me to my family's cabin in Priest Lake, Idaho for 2 - 3 weeks. This was the only time I ever took off from work, and I cherished it immensely, as did my sons. It also gave them an opportunity to develop relationships with my parents, my siblings and their cousins.

Fortunately, during the time I spent in the failed partnership, I had also continued with my own video business, and it grew and prospered rapidly. But I was missing out on the most lucrative assignments because my equipment was outdated. For starters, the camera I used was attached by a cable to the recording deck, and the format was known as 3/4 inch, better than VHS, but not nearly as good as a new format called Betacam. Cameras with built-in recorders, called camcorders, were now readily available.

I had to make a nerve-wracking decision: be content with where I was at, or take a giant leap and go all in. I chose the latter and purchased the best camera that was on the market, a Sony Betacam BVW-400. When it arrived, I held it in my hands and thought maybe I had made a mistake. What if things didn't work out? After all, I wasn't some big fancy production house with deep pocket investors.

The camera cost $38,500. I suddenly felt very alone.

4

Ups and Downs

My failed partnership and my second failed marriage left me feeling pensive. My mind went back to the craziness of when I had flown on a one-way ticket to Maui 15 years ago. I recalled all the jobs I had worked on for 10 years - at times five simultaneously - just to save enough money to risk working in a profession I knew nothing about. After owning a home, which was something I had never dreamed possible, it was now all gone. I was back to living in an apartment, and I had risked the proceeds from the house sale on upgrading my video equipment. What if the business didn't come in? What if this was a foolish decision? It was a frightening prospect.

Eventually, everything did work out in my business life. My personal life, however, continued to be a series of failed relationships. I got married for the third time, and we had a son Bryan who was born in 1994. But that marriage too ended the same way as my previous ones, and Bryan and his mom moved to, of all places, Connecticut. In the meantime, my eldest son Sean, who had been living in Connecticut with his mom, was now living with me on Maui.

I had weathered a major crisis in my business, and at least three emotional crises in my failed marriages, and if you had asked me how I was doing spiritually, I would have replied that I was a crisis Christian there as well. I only prayed when I wanted something, and just went to church on Christmas and Easter. I didn't really know if God even existed, and was worried that if He did, it probably meant that hell was real too. It was not something I wanted to think about, so I didn't. What I did know was that I definitely wasn't going to heaven, if it even existed, because I had fallen away from the only passage there - the Catholic religion.

One day Mike Knowles, a close friend of mine, invited me to attend his church service at Hope Chapel, where he volunteered as the audiovisual technician. I accepted his invitation, and during the singing was shocked to see everyone lifting their hands in the air and going crazy over Jesus. That was terribly irreverent in my opinion. Didn't they know that church was supposed to be a solemn affair? So I was 'one and done' and never went back.

But there was something about Mike Knowles' character that I admired. He was a video engineer, and I used to hire him periodically to fix or tweak my equipment. At times we would have an emergency situation, and I would be highly stressed, but he would have this calm assurance that all was okay, even when it definitely wasn't. His wife Mary used to have periodic seizures, but through it all, they never complained or felt sorry for themselves. While I was doing somersaults chasing a worldly dream, Mike's priority was first and foremost God, closely followed by his wife and their two daughters.

One thing that did have a profound effect on me spiritually was the video work I was periodically hired to do at Haggai Institute. This was a privately funded Christian Organization that would fly people to Maui from Third World countries, house and feed them during several weeks of biblical training, and then fly them back to minister in their home countries. I videotaped several of their training sessions, but the most inspiring were the personal interviews and the convocation ceremonies that I would see and hear as I worked.

Life continued pleasantly on, and I was now the owner of a beautiful home in Kula Kai, an exclusive residential neighborhood located on the slopes of Haleakala, Maui's 10,000-foot dormant volcano. One day, while Sean was sitting in the living room, I went onto the roof to wash off the solar panels. I can only imagine what Sean was thinking when he heard my footsteps on the roof because he knew that I would discover the marijuana plants he was secretly growing up there.

When I found them, I merely picked up each potted plant and dropped it from the roof, one at a time, right next to the window where I knew Sean was sitting. Splat! Splat! Splat! Splat! I then took my time washing off the solar panels, climbed back down the ladder and went into the house. I wasn't surprised that Sean wasn't there. I knew he'd be worried about what I was going to say. But I wasn't going to say anything at all. And I never did. The message had already been delivered via Airmail. There will be NO drugs in our house!

Oh, the irony of ironies. Only God knew that in a few short years our roles would be dramatically reversed.

5

Mom

Business was booming, and I was working nonstop seven days a week. Although I was as passionate about my profession as ever, maintaining a high level of excellence was beginning to wear me down mentally as well as physically. The only break I ever took was my annual 2 - 3 week summer vacation in Priest Lake, Idaho. Burnout was becoming a real probability.

So in 1998, I determined to retire by the time my son Kevin graduated from High School in 2005. I called it my 'Seven Year Plan.'

That same year in June I flew to Seattle to surprise my mom on Mother's Day, even though I had to fly back to Maui the very next day because of work. I had not been with my mom on Mother's Day in over twenty years, ever since coming to Maui - although I did spend a lot of time with her during my annual summer vacations at the family cabin in Idaho. However, this Mother's Day was extra special; it might be her last. My mom had cancer.

Mom was an only child. Her father, whom I had nicknamed 'Bopi" as a toddler, had been an incredible role model for me. He had spent a lot of time with me while growing up, and I never once heard him say one negative word about anything or anyone. Unfortunately, his wife (my grandmother) passed away when I was 3 years old. I am sure it would have benefited me greatly to witness their relationship.

Mom was always totally committed to our family. If I could use only one word to describe her, it would be 'love.' As I approached the front door, my mom spotted me out the kitchen window and immediately started crying. I spent one of the best days of my life with her that day.

In March of the following year, 1999, my brother called to inform me that our mom was probably going to pass away at any moment and he would let me know when the services would be held. I had no idea that she was that close to dying. I asked him to put her on the phone.

"Mom, I'm coming home to see you."

"Oh honey, you don't have to do that."

"You just hang in there."

"Ok."

It was spring break, and all the airlines were booked solid, so it took me five days to get on a flight. When my brother picked me up at the airport at 10 pm, I assumed we would spend the night at his home and then drive to my parents in the morning. But he took me straight there, telling me that I had better see her right away. I soon realized why. She was lying on a bed in the living room, barely breathing the oxygen fed through her nose. She could not have weighed more than 60 lbs.

I sat next to her, held her hand and read the two letters written by my sons Kevin and Sean which I had brought with me. She squeezed my hand gently whenever I began speaking, confirming that she was hearing me. Suddenly I found myself compelled to read from the oversized Bible that was always lying on the living room bookshelf. As far as I knew, no one in our family had ever opened it except maybe to look at the colorful pictures grouped in the middle. I opened it randomly, read some Scripture verses, didn't understand a thing I was reading, and put it down after a few minutes. It just seemed like the right thing to do, and I was glad that I had at least tried.

By now the rest of my family had either gone to bed or gone back to their homes. It was late, almost midnight. I leaned over close to my mom's ear and said softly, "Mom, it's ok, you can go now." I went to sleep next to her on the living room couch, and when I awoke at 6 am, she was gone.

Three days later, on a Friday afternoon, over 300 people attended my mom's Memorial Service. To have that size of a turnout, on such short notice and on a weekday, was a tribute to how many lives had been touched by my mom's love.

6

Living the Dream

My video business continued to grow and prosper. Cruise Control, a booking agency based in Maryland, was referring their Federal Government clients to me. Crew Connections, a booking agency based in Colorado, was referring their Network Television clients to me. Corporate convention shows were increasing through repeat business and advertising, and the wedding business was booming, averaging 30 - 40 weddings a month, which required my purchasing more equipment and training people as subcontractors to shoot and edit them.

By late 2001, I was solidly on track to achieve my goal of retiring by 2005. A friend and I purchased land in a gated community with bi-coastal views, and my brother-in-law drafted plans for the construction of a beautiful home. The future looked very promising indeed.

Then, in 2002, a wedding company I had serviced faithfully for almost three years reneged on an oral agreement we had made for future work. I felt betrayed. Not only had I purchased thousands of dollars' worth of equipment to service this company, but I had loyal friends who were working for me that I would no longer be able to use, and they were counting on me.

I sued for breach of contract. All I wanted was the wedding company to honor our agreement. Instead, they counter-sued me. This dragged on for a year, which really stressed me out. In the end, I just wanted it over with and agreed to their offer of merely paying the attorney's fees that I had accumulated, about $10,000.

However, as bad as that was, even more stressful for me during this time was an on-again/off-again relationship I was going through.

The dream I had been living soon became a nightmare.

7

Crack

Late one evening I was driving around aimlessly, guzzling beers in a fruitless attempt to drown my sorrows. I knew that my coping mechanism for what was bothering me was wrong, but I didn't care. Foolishly I picked up a hitchhiker who proceeded to introduce me to crack cocaine, and by the time the sun came up I was feeling rotten about myself. She begged me to make what would have been my third trip to an ATM to buy more crack, however I refused and drove home, swearing to myself I would never touch that stuff again.

A month later the phone rang, and to my surprise it was the woman hitchhiker, asking if I wanted to get together. Apparently I gave her my business card the night we met. By now the remorse I had felt from the first time had worn off. I agreed to see her. Another all-nighter ensued, and I again returned home feeling dirty, ashamed, and disgusted with myself. This drug scared me. I had to come up with a plan. I didn't want her to call again.

So the next day I cooked up a fictitious story that my physician had warned me I would have an aneurysm if I continued doing that stuff. I drove to where she was staying determined to give her this message. She wasn't there, so I left a note on her door. That night she called saying she had gotten the note, wished me well, and promised never to contact me again.

Two days later, I was desperately knocking on her door.

8

Addiction

My family has a history of alcoholism that goes back two generations that I know of, and more than likely, even farther. People born with this genetic predisposition are more susceptible to becoming alcoholics or addicts, just like people with a family history of heart disease in their bloodline are at higher risk of suffering a heart attack.

The surefire way to avoid alcoholism or addiction is to never take that first drink or do that first drug because you're playing Russian roulette. If you squeeze off the chamber loaded with the particular substance you are genetically predisposed to getting addicted to, you're a goner.

I know and wholeheartedly agree that experimenting with any drug is foolish and wrong. Though I must confess that in my teens and early adulthood I had used a variety of illegal substances, but I had always been able to quit without any problem. Because of this, I had a false impression that walking away from any substance would always be easy.

I fired the fatal bullet when I tried crack, not realizing a seed of destruction had already been genetically planted. I was 50 years old. After using that second time, my life immediately spiraled entirely out of control. I lived to use and, worse yet, used to live. The cravings were insatiable.

I was hired as a cameraman on the Golf Channel's' studio set for the Mercedes Golf Tournament in Kapalua, Maui. At the same tournament, I was also shooting Sports coverage on the golf course for the local network affiliates. As soon as we wrapped each day, I would race to the other end of the island and smoke crack until it was time to return to the job site the next morning. This madness went on for four days; not sleeping, not showering, not even changing clothes. I was totally strung out, sweating profusely and smelling like death warmed over on the job site. I had worked at this tournament for several years. This time would be my last.

One day while I was at home I ran out of crack. I phoned a dealer, and he told me on the phone I had thirty minutes to pick it up. I raced down the mountain on my Harley Davidson in a panic. Hitting loose gravel on a sharp turn, I sheared off the road, slammed into a boulder and flew over the handlebars. It was a miracle I didn't break my neck or back, or even worse, die. People came rushing out of a house saying they'd call an ambulance. 'No way!' I thought. I crawled over to the bike, and with the handlebars bent sideways, and a shattered headlight, I sputtered to my destination.

Over the next two days, I couldn't even move or get out of bed from the trauma my body had suffered in that crash. Finally, on the third day when I was barely able to stand up, and scared that I might have internal injuries, I went to a doctor. They checked me out and took blood samples. A couple of days later I went back for a follow-up exam. The doctor said I would be OK, but, based on the results from my blood sample and without being specific, also told me that I did have a problem. We both knew what that was. I said I'd get help.

I didn't.

9

A Call for Help

As my addiction consumed me, it was only a matter of time before my son Sean, now 21 years old, would find out. The extent to which he did everything humanly possible to get me to quit is a heart-wrenching testament of a son's love for his dad.

When Sean first confronted me, I didn't deny my drug use. But when he declared that I needed to go into rehab, I went into complete denial. I insisted that I didn't have a problem and promised to quit.

How could I deny that I had a serious problem when it was so obvious that I did? Was I lying? No. I honestly believed that I didn't. Why? Because the addicted part of me was terrified of quitting. Later on, I would learn that this is one of the stages of addiction – denial of the problem and powerlessness in overcoming it. By the time I did realize I was an addict, hopelessness and despair had taken root, and the only remedy was to continue to self-medicate.

As time went by and my condition worsened, I began to stay away from the home I owned in Kula Kai as much as possible because Sean was living with me there. In desperation, my son called my family on the Mainland, asking for help. I had been hiding out at a friend's house for over a week, smoking crack nonstop, when one day I thought I heard what sounded like familiar voices outside the front door. I looked out a window, and to my horror, saw two of my sisters, and my dad! Meanwhile, Sean climbed through another window and found me.

I went to the door with Sean and promised everyone I would come home in two hours. Sean voiced his doubts about me actually showing up. But the fact that my family had flown all the way from Seattle to Maui, and Sean had somehow found where I was hanging out; well, I had to follow through on this promise.

I was extremely nervous about how my dad would treat me when I got to my house. Amazingly, he was kind and compassionate. It was a side of him I hardly knew existed, and I especially didn't expect it under these circumstances. In embarrassment, I admitted to them the obvious, that I had a drug problem, and thanked them for responding to my son's request for help in getting me straightened out.

While they lodged for a week at an inexpensive hotel in Kahului near the airport, I managed to stay clean and remained at home the entire time they were on Maui. My dad offered to stay indefinitely at our house on Maui with Sean and me, to be sure I could keep it together. I thanked him and told him everything would be ok now, not to worry, no need to stay.

We said our goodbyes at the airport, and as I drove away,

I called my drug dealer and bought some crack, and then stayed away from my home for several days. Finally, I had to get a change of clothes, but I didn't want to be confronted by my son, so I drove past our house to be sure his truck wasn't in the driveway. When I saw the coast was clear, I parked and ran into our home, grabbed what I needed, and ran back out to my car. Before I could get in, Sean drove up in his truck.

"Dad, give me the drugs," he said as he stepped out of his truck.

"I don't have any," I replied.

"Yes you do," he said, as he walked toward me.

"No, I don't," I said, backpedaling away from him. By now I was in the middle of the street.

Sean thrust his hand down my pants pocket and pulled out my bag of crack.

"It's not you that's lying to me, dad. It's the drugs."

I just stood staring at the ground, feeling sorry for myself that he had taken what I desperately needed.

"Why can't you just quit?" He asked.

Looking up at him, all I could say was, "I wish I could." And I meant it.

We walked into our home, and I slumped in a chair, utterly defeated, as Sean called my family and made arrangements to get me into rehab. The next day I was on a plane to Seattle.

My dad met me at the airport and drove me straight to the rehab facility which was located in Kirkland, a suburb of Seattle. It was a 28-day inpatient program, meaning all the participants lived and stayed on the property. I'm not sure what our expectations were. Would this cure my addiction?

I was soon informed that there was no cure. The purpose of rehab was to help the addict/alcoholic manage their addictions utilizing the Twelve Steps of AA.

Almost all the men and women in the program were there involuntarily, ordered by the court, after being arrested on drug and/or alcohol-related offenses. So they had no choice. I was one of the few exceptions, someone who had voluntarily entered rehab. For an addict, there was nothing more terrifying than denying oneself the opportunity to get high. Continuing to use, however, would inevitably lead to one of three possible endings: death, suicide, or institutions (prison and insane asylums).

I was in pretty bad shape upon arrival. I hadn't slept or eaten much in quite a while. My brain was frazzled, and I had lost a lot of weight. I began to eat like a horse and after about three days was playing basketball and feeling much better physically. My family was very supportive and attended group sessions when they were allowed to. The days, however, seemed to me like months, and my head began coming up with all kinds of excuses to leave.

On the 10th day, I told my dad when he came out for a visit that I was going back to Maui because I couldn't be away from my video business any longer.

"You just don't have the guts" he snarled, with a mean look that had terrified me many times when I was a little boy. I got angry and told him to leave.

The next day I took a taxi to SeaTac airport and flew back to Maui.

10

Downward Spiral

I arrived home determined to stay clean. My son was skeptical, and rightfully so. After all, I had bailed out of a 28-day rehab program after only 10 days. So he took a week off from work to stay with me at the house. The following week he returned to work, but before driving away, he asked me to give him the keys to my car. No sense in taking the chance on me running off again while he was away. I totally agreed.

And it worked - for two days. I then called a locksmith.

"Thanks for coming," I said as he arrived. "I need you to make a set of keys for my car."

"Well, that could be a problem," said the locksmith.

"What do you mean 'a problem'?" I asked.

"Your son says not to make you any keys," he said.

I was incredulous! There are dozens of locksmiths on Maui. None of this made any sense. How could this be happening?

"But it's my car," I pleaded.

"Well, your son says you have a drinking problem, and if I make you a set of keys and you get in an accident, he will hold me liable."

That was nice of my son, I thought, as I stood there with my mouth wide open, trying to formulate a response. At least he didn't tell the locksmith that I was a full-on crack-head. But before I could come up with any further argument, and I was determined to do just that, the locksmith dropped the final bomb:

"Look, your son is on his way here now. Why don't we just wait for him and figure this out when he gets here?"

Now I was really freaked out, and the intense craving to get high was raging inside of me.

"That's OK," I said to the locksmith, "you can go."

As soon as he left, I started walking, hating myself every step of the way for what I was putting my son through, yet too consumed by my failure to overcome my addiction to do anything about it. Several days later, after having stayed away from my home smoking crack non-stop since the encounter with the locksmith, my son spotted me sitting on a bench outside a grocery store.

"What are you doing, dad?"

"Nothing, just hanging out."

"I'm taking you home. Wait here, I'll be right back."

As soon as my son walked into the store I bolted to the parking lot and hopped into the Jeep I had been riding in. The driver was one of my drug suppliers.

"My son just spotted me. Get out of here fast."

We drove out of the parking lot and headed down Haleakala Highway, when all of a sudden I felt something bump the back of the jeep.

"What was that?" I asked the driver.

"Your son! He's right behind us!"

Sean continued to bump us with his truck until we had to come to a stop in a line of cars at a red light. Then he hopped out of his truck, ran to the driver's side of the jeep and started throwing punches through the open window at the driver, yelling: "What are you doing to my dad? What are you doing to my dad?"

The light turned green, and we drove off, leaving my son standing there in the middle of the road. When the driver started to rant at me about what had just happened, I cut him off.

"What do you expect him to do? He's my son!" I screamed, my heart breaking.

11

Aruba

My work was the least of my concerns. In fact, it was a nuisance that had to be discarded. I didn't see any hope of getting clean, and I was too frazzled to run my company any longer, so I stopped accepting any new work and began canceling jobs that were already scheduled.

There were, however, two upcoming projects that I couldn't avoid. Both were week-long convention shows for clients I had serviced in the past, before my addiction. The first was for a pharmaceutical company staying at a resort in Wailea on Maui. I was a complete mess, bouncing between being high on crack, and suffering from withdrawal when I wasn't. I wouldn't even let Sean, who was assisting me, into my hotel room, because it was littered with drug paraphernalia.

"Dad, don't you know everyone here can tell what you're doing?" He pleaded, embarrassed for me. He was pointing out the obvious, and knowing this only added to my paranoia. I was living a nightmare. I couldn't stop.

I . . . just . . . couldn't . . . STOP!

After shooting each day, I would go up to my Editor's room to assist with the editing, just like we had done during many conventions in the past. But now I was no help at all. I would just curl up in a chair, with my head spinning, hating my life. Fortunately, my Editor, who was a good friend and very talented, salvaged the project. It was completed as scheduled in time for the group to view on the last day of their trip.

Next up was a software company based in California. I had previously produced two shows for them, one on Maui and one on the island of Kauai. This year they were going to Aruba, and the video highlights would be shown a few months later at a meeting of the entire Sales force back in the States as an incentive to qualify for next year's trip. This meant I didn't have to worry about editing until we returned to Maui. I was truly honored that they would fly Sean and I half-way around the globe to cover this event.

I had received their convention itinerary in advance of our arrival, so I had the shots, skits, sound bites, music, special effects and so on, all choreographed in what was left of my mind before we started. This was a challenging assignment; it's always tougher when you are racing around trying to capture everything at a location you are unfamiliar with. On some days, multiple activities and events were happening simultaneously in various parts of the island, and we needed to include all of them in the final product. Thankfully, we were able to accomplish all of our objectives successfully.

The trip to Aruba was a wonderful experience; spending quality time with my son, just like the old days before I became an addict. Being away from Maui and my easily accessible drug contacts helped keep my mind off of using for the first time in months. I really did want to get well. But, realistically, I didn't see that happening on Maui.

The Aruba trip gave me a glimmer of hope, that maybe if I moved away from Maui, I could get clean and stay clean; set free from the daily battle I was fighting and losing. It would be worth trying.

I was desperate.

12

Insanity

As soon as Sean and I returned to Maui, I put both my house and the land I had purchased with my friend in the gated community up for sale. I intended to move permanently back to the Mainland as soon as either one sold. In the meantime, with my Video Productions company basically shut down, I disappeared for several weeks.

My addiction was hell-bent on going out in flames. I went days without sleeping or eating; crashing and burning, then repeating the cycle. My body wasted away, my mind turned to mush. As my tolerance increased, the highs weren't as intense and subsided too quickly. To counter this, I had to increase both the quantity and frequency I was smoking crack to avoid the agonizing, brutal depression of coming down.

I lived in constant paranoia and began hallucinating. One night I was in a vacant lot for hours, crawling on my stomach around a building that didn't exist, fearful of the Swat team that had me surrounded. Of course, they didn't exist either. Another night I scrambled down into a ravine to escape what I thought was an entire army after me. I stayed down there until dawn, listening to them talk about me. I was a bloody, muddy mess by the time I stumbled home; shirt and shorts torn, scrapes covering my arms and legs.

I was going insane.

Then one day I snuck back into our home just to take a shower, hoping to get away before my son showed up. Before I could leave, Sean walked through the front door. Taking me by the hand, Sean led me into the bathroom and stood me in front of the mirror.

"Dad, look at yourself," he said plaintively.

I wasn't horrified by what I saw, only resigned to my self-destruction. Hollow eyes, varicose veins, skin and bones – I was 6'2", 125lbs of approaching death. My son, standing next to me, was crying. I slowly turned around, went to my bed, and laid down. Sean laid next to me and put his arm over me. When I awoke in the morning, he was gone to work.

I went back out.

13

2003

The vacant lot sold and arrangements were made to get me off the island as quickly as possible. When I met with the Realtor who purchased the lot, I broke down sobbing. "I just want to get well," I cried.

The day before my scheduled departure I left home and started walking to a house where I had been doing drugs with a woman I had been hanging out with. It was about a mile away, and the only road there was the same road my son would be traveling coming home from work. Knowing this made me super paranoid. I was desperate to get high, and I didn't want him to catch me on the road, so I kept hiding behind bushes and lying in ditches along the way.

Sure enough, as I stumbled along the road between hiding places, here came Sean's little orange Toyota truck. Stopping next to me, he sees the small shaving kit bag I'm carrying containing my drug paraphernalia, and asks me to give it to him. As I hand it to him through the driver's side window, he tells me to hop in the truck. I plead with him to let me go, that it's my last night.

I start walking down the road, hoping he won't check my pockets. However, Sean gets out, runs up and wraps his arms around me, trying to get me back to his truck. I see a car approaching and purposely flop to the ground.

"Help! Help!" I scream hysterically.

"What's going on?" Someone yells as the car comes to a stop.

"None of your business!" My son yells at them. By now another car had stopped, and I got up and started walking again. Behind me, I could hear arguing.

"My dad is a drug addict!" Sean finally yells at them in frustration, then gets into his truck and heads home, leaving me to my misery.

Early the next morning, Sean showed up where I was staying. My son Kevin's mom and her husband were with him to help in case there was any reluctance on my part. There wasn't, I was resigned and ready, and very appreciative of their support. Back at my home, they helped me pack, then drove me to the airport. Arrangements were made for my dad to meet me when I arrived in Seattle. I would be staying with him and immediately begin intensive outpatient rehab.

The year was 2003.

14

Starting Over

I was 52 years old when I moved back into my childhood bedroom, and it was quite a humbling experience. I could easily afford to rent my own apartment, but I knew I needed to be accountable to someone, to be kept "in check" so to speak. Even though my relationship with my dad was strained by past hurts and recent disappointments, I knew I couldn't trust myself. I was grateful, yet fearful.

The 28-day outpatient care program began immediately. I was required to attend two-hour nightly group sessions Monday through Friday. It was kind of like being back in school, and I enjoyed it. My mind was scrambled when I left Maui, and now I was slowly beginning to think normally again.

I was also gradually beginning to feel better physically. It's amazing what sleep and food can do for your body; I had little of either during the past two years of my addiction.

For the first three weeks, everything went well. Then the

lady friend I had been drugging with on Maui made plans to move to the Mainland. I knew that moving out of my dad's home would jeopardize my recovery, so I asked him if she could live with us. He said no.

When she arrived, we checked into an upscale hotel close to where my outpatient classes were being held. After I successfully completed the program, we rented an apartment together. The inevitable happened: We started smoking crack again.

This went on for a couple of weeks. Then I packed the SUV I purchased and drove alone to my dad's house, hoping he would let me move back in. I dreaded having to grovel, and I was extremely nervous about his reaction to my relapse. But, I was desperate to get back on track. The month of sobriety, while enrolled in the outpatient program, had given me hope.

My dad was a master at knowing what words would cut the deepest, and he was at the top of his game as soon as I walked through the front door. Finally, I just said:

"You can help me out - or kick me out."

When his verbal abuse continued unabated, I walked out to my car and drove away.

15

Clueless in Seattle

The desperation that had led me to seek asylum at my dad's house quickly wore off. In Seattle, I checked into a seedy, crack infested motel and got caught up in a very dark world. Initially, I thought the people who came to my room were my friends. They would warn me to keep the drapes shut and not to go out because it was too dangerous. But in reality, they just wanted to hide me from everyone else. I was the only one who had money. I was the only one paying for everything.

They freaked out when on the fifth day, at around 2 am, I opened the door and walked outside. Looking around, I saw a group of people huddled at a bus stop across the street. I figured it was where a lot of the drug dealing took place, so I walked over.

"Hey, I was wondering if I could apply for a job as a look-out, then move into Sales and eventually become Director of Marketing," I asked these total strangers with a straight face.

They looked at me, I looked at them, and after a moment of awkward silence, I handed each of them some crack.

"Just joking," I said.

Sure, it was a stupid thing to do. I could have been shot, but I didn't care. I didn't care about anything. Whatever remorse I had felt early on in my addiction was now completely gone. I was a drug addict, that was what I would always be, and in my twisted mind that was okay, as long as I didn't hurt anyone other than myself.

When my house on Maui sold, I had all my furniture and belongings shipped to a house I was renting in Bellevue. But I hardly ever stayed there, preferring instead to hang with the motel crazies. The daily drama was intoxicating; entertaining in a sick sort of way.

In reality, it was a ruthless, perverted, insane world, populated by penniless drug addicts desperate to get high. I was beaten, robbed several times, and had a pistol pressed against my forehead. Twice I was kidnapped and held for ransom. My cars were stolen (one on the same day I purchased it!) and wrecked. My house was burglarized and ransacked.

I was 'put out', as they say on the streets, many times (a term referring to knucklehead, naïve addicts like myself who, when they are in someone's room paying for everyone's drugs and then run out of money, find that they're no longer welcome, and are told to leave).

Broke and destitute, something good finally happened to me: I got arrested and thrown into jail.

16

Jail

Ah, it's finally over, I thought to myself, as I rode in the back of the police car. I was safe from the misery, chaos, and insanity. I hadn't slept or eaten in what seemed like forever, and I remember thinking how wonderful it would be if I rolled up on my bunk and never woke up.

I was charged with two misdemeanors: trespassing and criminal mischief. On the third day of my incarceration, I had my first court appearance. The public defender assigned to me told me that since I had a clean record, I would be sentenced for time served and released that day if I pleaded guilty. I said "No way," and pleaded not guilty. The judge then set my next court appearance for a week later.

I returned to my jail cell angry and bitter toward the person who had called the police on me. I couldn't imagine being in jail for another week. I was desperate to get out, to get high, to get revenge. I called my dad to see if he'd bail me out. Nope.

"Get off drugs," he said in a dry monotone.

Then one of my sisters grabbed the phone from him. I pleaded my case, and tried to make her understand that I was really having a horrible time dealing with my addiction and that I didn't want to be this way. I wasn't looking for sympathy, just understanding. She cut me off.

"I've read the book. You're nothing but a f***ing drug addict," she spat.

'What book?' I thought. Obviously not the one written by The American Medical Association that states addiction is a chronic brain disease and not a character disorder. At any rate, my family made it clear they didn't want to have anything to do with me. This only caused me to become more angry and bitter.

To make matters worse, for some unknown reason my Public Defender got changed, causing my next court appearance to be moved to an even later date. I decided to change my plea to guilty. I wanted to do whatever it took to get out of there. But I couldn't get ahold of my new Public Defender. In fact, I couldn't even find out who it was! Over the next few days, I just sat around with the other inmates playing cards and dominoes, not knowing what to think, trying not to think.

Then one day while sitting alone, feeling that my situation was hopeless and my life worthless, my attention was drawn to a small group of men huddled in an outer courtyard. Two of them were dressed in normal attire. I wondered what was going on. Something inside of me prompted me to go find out.

When I did, my life was changed forever.

17

"Yes, I need Jesus"

I walked out to the courtyard and asked curiously, "What's going on?"

One of the young men wearing normal clothes came up to me. He looked like he was in his mid-twenties, fresh-faced and eager.

"We're talking about Jesus. Would you like Jesus to come into your life?"

Into my life? Jesus? What on earth did that mean? I had turned my back on the Catholic religion, so why would Jesus want to come into my life? How could He still want to have anything to do with me after I had been such a huge disappointment to Him, to my sons, and to myself?

But there was something in this young man's eyes that emanated truth and hope. Suddenly, without warning, a flood of tears bursted from my eyes.

"Yes," I sobbed, "I need Jesus."

He put his hand on my shoulder. "Ok, I am going to lead you in prayer. Just repeat each line after me." As my tears continued to flow, I nodded, and we prayed.

"Dear God, I come to you confessing that I am a sinner. I believe that Jesus came to earth and was crucified on a cross for me and my sins, and rose from the dead that I too might have eternal life. Dear God, I surrender my life to You. Please help me to be what You want me to be. Thank You for saving me and accepting me. In Jesus' name, I pray. Amen."

I remember talking with him for a few more minutes after we prayed, however I can't recall what was said. I walked slowly back into the main room feeling a bit strange, but in a nice kind of way. Even today it's hard to explain, but there was an unfamiliar lightness inside of me. It was as though something dark and heavy had been removed.

I soon realized it was more than a feeling. In some intangible way, I was a changed man with a new attitude and fresh hopes. I had come to jail an angry, bitter, dazed and confused wreck, but now an overwhelming peace and comfort suffused me. All my bitterness and anger were entirely gone.

I immediately experienced an unfamiliar and urgent desire to find a Bible and start reading it. I discovered that I LOVED it! A pastor came the next day to invite us to attend a Bible study. I eagerly accepted the invitation. There was so much I didn't know or understand - which was basically everything. I still remember my first question: "Why does God need us to praise Him?" I asked, wondering if God had an ego issue.

"That's a great question," he responded. "God doesn't actually need our praise."

'Huh?,' that doesn't make sense, I thought, recalling the

verses I had been reading in the Bible the night before about praising God for all kinds of stuff.

The pastor continued, “God wants us to praise Him for our benefit, not His. Praising Him focuses our attention on Him; on His goodness, mercy, forgiveness, grace, faithfulness, love, and power, rather than focusing our attention on our circumstances.”

Wow. I had so much to learn. The religion I had been raised in was all about tradition and rituals - those I knew - but this God I didn’t know at all.

Then an amazing thing happened, something I had never remotely considered. I suddenly felt a strong urge to begin writing a letter of reconciliation to my dad. How weird is that!? I had grown so accustomed to hating my dad, and in my mind he deserved it. I owned this hatred, and no one was ever going to take it from me.

Yet here I was, feeling that writing him a letter was the most natural thing to do, like breathing. Words and thoughts started coming into my mind faster than I could write them down. One page, two pages, three pages, four, five, six, and, without realizing it, I was just getting warmed up!

This went on for days, and the other inmates started giving me a hard time about it, but I ignored them. All, that is, except the one who said to me:

“Your dad did the best that he could.”

That statement really struck a chord, a chord that the old Scott would have dismissed instantly. Now I took it to heart and began pondering on how hard it must have been for my dad to show affection, considering that he had been sent off to live with relatives as a young child. I had always compared him unfavorably with my friend’s dads, but that wasn’t fair.

The letter contained every grievance I could think of, all my failings, lots of Bible verses, and, most importantly, a desire to forgive and move forward. It was 28 pages long when I finally mailed it out. I discovered, to my delight, that the hate I dragged around my entire life had disappeared entirely.

I asked my dad a couple of months later if he had received my letter. His only remark was that I had a good memory. 'Too funny,' I thought. I was just happy that he had actually read it.

The day after mailing the letter to my dad, I was called into court. The sister who had cursed me on the phone was sitting in the back of the courtroom, so I figured maybe she had a change of heart and was there in a supportive role. At any rate, I pleaded guilty and was released at 7am the following day, my 28th day of being locked up.

How ironic, 28 - the same number of days as the number of pages I wrote in the letter to my dad. I thought that was kind of neat, to be honest. God had kept me in jail just long enough to get that letter written, and not a day longer.

So, now what . . . ?

18

Now What?

It was a cold, dark, rainy October day when I walked out the back door of the Pierce County Jail in Tacoma, Washington. When I was arrested 28 days earlier, I had been barefoot and was wearing dirty jeans and a torn t-shirt. They had kept my unwashed clothes in a bag for all those days. I stunk. Thankfully they didn't let me walk out barefoot; I was allowed to keep my jail-issued pink slippers, although wearing them in public was quite embarrassing.

I didn't know anyone in Tacoma except my sister I had seen in the courtroom, the same sister who had cussed me out on the phone. I was destitute, and definitely looked it. After almost a full month of sobriety and a renewed faith in God, I had hope that I could now begin rebuilding my life. But I needed a place to stay, so I walked around until I found a payphone, panhandled some change, and called my sister.

"Uh, hi, this is Scott. I just got out of jail."

"I know that," she replied in a cold, unfriendly tone.

I immediately realized she had not come to court to support me, only to keep tabs on me.

"Well, I don't have anywhere to go and was wondering …"

She cut me off before I could continue.

"You're not coming here."

I paused, not knowing what to say.

"Well, could you give me a ride?" I finally asked.

"Where to?" She snapped.

"I guess to the dealership that has my car" I answered, though I doubted they would give it to me. I owned it free and clear, but they had taken it over a dispute regarding damages to another car they had loaned me while mine was in for repairs. Ugh. My life was such a mess.

"Where are you? I'll send my husband."

I gave her the address, and her husband arrived about a half hour later. He took me to the dealership, gave me a few dollars, and then drove off. I wasn't surprised when the dealership refused to release my car. Stranded once again, the only place I could think of going now was 25 miles away. So I began walking and stressing the whole way there, because it was a place I had done a lot of drugs at, and I didn't want to fall back into that lifestyle. But, I didn't know where else to go.

When I finally got there, all I wanted to do was talk about Jesus. I was rebuffed. So, I asked if I could stay in the garage, away from the main house, away from the bad memories, and was told that would be ok. After a week of feeling depressed and worrying about relapsing, I walked 5 miles to the nearest pay phone and called a different sister. I told her of my concerns and asked if she would come to the store and take me to a friend's house near the small town of Carnation, about 40 miles northeast of Seattle. This friend was a former High School classmate, and I knew she wasn't a druggie.

My sister came out and took me there. I hadn't called my friend in advance and didn't know if it would be alright to stay with her. I only knew I had to get away from where I was. Fortunately, she allowed me in, and right away I started talking about Jesus, but she wasn't interested either. At least she allowed me to stay, and I began enjoying the first normal living situation I had experienced in quite some time; peaceful, no drama, no drugs. However, the desire to use was with me every minute of every day, and, in a sick sort of way, I missed the motel craziness. Such is the nature of addiction.

† † †

My friend helped me sell one of my cameras on eBay. With part of the proceeds I purchased a round-trip airline ticket to Palm Springs so I could visit my youngest son, Bryan. He was about nine years old at the time, and I hadn't seen him since he was five.

My friend dropped me off at SeaTac airport, and as soon as she drove off, I walked to one of the motels I used to frequent, relapsed, and missed my flight.

How could this have happened, you may ask? Wasn't my new found faith genuine? It certainly was, and Brennan Manning, in his book "The Ragamuffin Gospel," explains it this way:

> *Often I have been asked, "Brennan, how is it possible that you became an alcoholic after you were saved?" It is possible because I got battered*

> *and bruised by loneliness and failure; because I got discouraged, uncertain, guilt-ridden, and took my eyes off of Jesus. Because my Christ encounter did not transfigure me into an angel. Because justification by grace through faith means I am set in right relationship with God, not made equivalent of a patient etherized on a table.*[1]

In my case, all I can say is this: I was an addict when I went into jail, a Christian addict when I came out.

The day after my relapse, full of remorse, I called my son's mom. She was rightfully upset with me and said I couldn't come now that I had let Bryan down. I felt horrible about hurting my son's feelings, and offered her a thousand dollars if she would let me fly out that day. She agreed.

I then called my friend I was staying with because she was holding the rest of my money from the camera sale. Understandably, she too got upset about my relapse, but drove out and met me at the airport with a check made out to my son's mom.

I was in Palm Springs for only a few days, but it was great to be there for Bryan. I knew it wasn't right that he should wonder why his dad wasn't always there for him, and whether his dad really cared. He couldn't have known that when I was away from him, I always felt grief and guilt every time I saw a boy his age.

Now was the time I could begin making amends.

[1] *The Ragamuffin Gospel*, by Brennan Manning, Multnomah Books, 2015. pp.30-31

19

Splat! Hitting Rock Bottom

The anticipation of getting high began to build as soon as I boarded the plane back to Seattle. Addiction is an opportunistic demon, it plays with your mind and strikes hardest when you are most vulnerable. I was supposed to call the friend I was living with to come and pick me up when I landed, but that would be an opportunity lost. I still had money left over from the trip in my pocket. I walked to the motels.

And was broke within two days.

I managed to get a ride with two guys back to where I was living. The plan was to pick up a $170 refund check I had left there, cash it, and return back to the motel together. When we got close to the house, I had them park about a block away. I didn't trust these people, and I definitely didn't want to jeopardize my friend's safety by letting them know where she lived.

I walked to the house dreading her anger and disappointment, but surprisingly, she broke down in tears and asked me why I was doing this to myself. She then offered to let me stay, on the condition that this would be my last chance. So I signed the refund check over to her, walked back to the car, gave the driver $150 cash and sent them on their way.

I was grateful to my friend and sincerely relieved to not be in that car heading back to the motels. Over the next couple of weeks, I did a lot of work around her property to fight off boredom and depression. I wrote an email to the car dealership, apologizing for all the mishaps, and asked if we could work something out regarding my car they were holding in lieu of the damages they claimed. I had originally purchased a brand new Volvo SUV for $48,000 cash from them when I had first arrived from Maui. Now they offered to give me a 1997 Volvo station wagon valued at $3500.

The friend I was living with gave me a ride to the dealership, and my intention was to drive straight back to her house. But, with $80 in my pocket from doing yard work for her neighbor, I found myself again at the motels and broke within a couple of hours. I then called the escrow company that had handled the sale of my house and found out there was some withheld money that I could collect. Within a week I received a check for $18,000.

I deposited the check at a check cashing business where they informed me it would take a few days until they had the funds, but fronted me $1000. I went straight to the motels, blew that money and went back begging for another $1000.

The next day, back at the motels, my station wagon was stolen.

When the funds came in, I had two people drive me to the check cashing place. I divided the money into two envelopes, and a day later both envelopes were stolen. I managed to find one of the envelopes in the trunk of their car that I had ridden in to the check cashing joint. I walked to a 7/11 store, saw a man and a woman sitting in a vehicle, obvious druggies, and offered them $100 to take me anywhere. I hopped in the back seat, alone, and we drove off.

All of a sudden, without warning, I started bawling. The people in the front seat turned around and asked me what was wrong, but I just ignored them. Up until then, I had suppressed the anguish of losing everything I had worked so hard for, and for my failure as a father. But now it all just erupted, and I continued to wail uncontrollably.

We ended up going to someone's house, a place I had never been before. They asked me how long I had been up without sleep, and I said several days. They offered me a glass of water, and the next thing I knew, I was laying on a bed, one day later. My last memory was drinking that glass of water. I looked down and saw that my pants pocket which held the envelope with my last $8000 had been cut open.

I stumbled outside and shuffled down an unfamiliar street, one foot barely making it front of the other, not knowing where I was going, not caring. No money, no car, no nothing. Despair was my only companion.

I had hit rock bottom.

20

New Life Program

After wandering aimlessly for several hours throughout South Seattle, I somehow found someone who allowed me to sleep at their apartment. The next day I decided to call my dad. I can't really say what prompted me, but it was easier to reach out now that I no longer felt any animosity toward him.

It's a good thing that I called him. He told me that my sister who lived in Tacoma had mentioned to him that there was a nine-month, live-in rehab program located at the Tacoma Rescue Mission. Better yet, it was free. Best of all, as I found out when I called the number he gave me, it was a Christian program. That sealed the deal for me. I was excited to start!

I called my dad back, and he said he'd drive me to Tacoma to fill out an application. Our first stop was the police station to file a stolen car report for my Volvo station wagon. We then drove to a pawn shop, and my dad paid $200 so I could retrieve an $1800 microphone I had pawned. When we finally arrived at the Tacoma Rescue Mission, I filled out an enrollment application for the New Life Program. They put my name on a waiting list and told me it would be 3 - 4 weeks before a bed would open up, but that I could sleep at their attached men's homeless shelter in the meantime.

At 6:30am every morning we were served breakfast, then sent out from the shelter to 'kick rocks'; slang for wandering aimlessly around town until we were allowed back in for the evening. I decided to spend my days at the Tacoma Library. At noon I would walk to a ministry that fed lunch to the homeless. Dinners were served back at the Mission. After three long weeks of this, I was finally admitted into the New Life Program in February of 2005.

All the participants were assigned jobs. I worked in the kitchen, primarily as a dishwasher. We served breakfast to about 150 homeless each morning, and dinner to nearly 300. After breakfast, we would attend a Bible Study facilitated by visiting pastors, staff and program participants. What a relief it was to learn that the people in the Bible weren't perfect as I had always thought, yet God worked mightily in and through them. I now believed that He would do the same for me if I allowed Him to.

During the day we would attend classes. My favorite was S.O.A.P class. We would choose a Scripture verse (S), write an Observation (O), write an Application (A), and write a Prayer (P).

Every night we would circle up for prayer, and on Sundays attend the church of our choice. I went to Champions Center where I was able to volunteer as a camera operator. Eventually, I was baptized there as well. I contacted Mike Knowles, my Christian friend who had taken me to the church service on Maui, to let him know how I was doing. He was thrilled, and informed me that his family had never stopped praying for me. I was very grateful to hear that, knowing their prayers played a significant part in how I came to know Jesus.

A couple of developments were happening outside the program as well. The police had located my stolen vehicle in Sacramento, California, and my dad flew down and drove it back up to Seattle. Also, my landlord at the house I had rented in Bellevue had moved everything I had shipped from Maui into storage, so my dad rented a truck and I went with him to retrieve it and take it to his house. When we opened the door to the storage unit, I was dismayed to see only a few boxes and one piece of video equipment. Everything else had been stolen. The boxes contained all the photographs of my kids, so for that I was grateful.

I was in the program six and a half months, everything was going smoothly, and then they moved someone who was difficult to get along with into my room. I wasn't happy about this and pulled an attitude, refusing to work or go to class unless they moved him or me to a different room. I was told this was unacceptable and that I would have to work it out. My new roommate had already been moved several times, and they were tired of dealing with this problem, so I was stuck with him.

Stubbornly, I stood firm in my decision not to do anything

unless one of us was moved, and was soon called into the Reverend's office and informed that I would have to leave the program. The Reverend felt bad for me, but I assured him I would be ok.

I wasn't. Within an hour of driving away, I relapsed.

21

Deja Vu

I know it sounds strange, but I really did think I was going to be alright when I left the program. Relapsing caught me by surprise. I didn't plan for it nor did I want it. But, I was now caught up in that dark world again, and I hated it.

I was out for about a month before I made my way back to the Mission, asking if I could apply to get back into the New Life Program. They agreed to let me in as soon as there was an opening, and put my name at the top of the waiting list. I spent the next two weeks 'kicking rocks' between the Mission's homeless shelter and the library, stayed clean and sober, and began the program for the second time in September of 2005.

The following month I attended the graduation ceremony for the group I had been a part of the first time around. Of the fifteen who had started in that group, only six had completed the entire nine months. That's about the norm and, unfortunately, so is relapsing for many of those who do graduate. It was an inspiring and emotional event. I was really happy for those who had graduated and felt sorry that I wasn't graduating with them.

This time around I was assigned janitorial work. I also helped out in the kitchen, the Donations Center, and anywhere else that I was needed. In the Challenge Learning Center, I volunteered as a tutor, helping people who hadn't graduated from high school to get their GED's.

And, once again, I dove into the curriculum, loving every bit of it and getting to know and understand God's nature through His written Word.

In May of 2006, I completed the nine-month program, along with five others from the original twenty who had started with me in September. My dad graciously told me I could stay with him, so I loaded up my Volvo station wagon and headed to his house outside Seattle.

I never made it there. Within an hour, the $60 in my pocket was gone. And so was my Volvo.

22

Recovery

Once you're addicted to crack, the desire for the euphoric high from a hit of that evil drug is an addict's constant nemesis. Rehab only helps in combating this desire; it's a daily battle to stay clean, a never-ending life-long war. There is no known cure for addiction or alcoholism. You're either actively using, or you're in recovery fighting the urge to use. That's just the way it is, and always will be.

I'm not making excuses for my relapses. Nothing forced me to relapse. But now, once again, I had lost the battle. If my car hadn't been stolen, I might have stayed out much longer, so that was a blessing in disguise. I hoped my dad would have mercy on me and still let me live at his house, considering I had just completed the full nine-month program. However, I was too nervous to call and ask him to come fetch me. So, I first called one of my sisters, explained and apologized for what happened, and asked if she would come get me and take me to his house. She said she would. I then called my dad, told him I was sorry and didn't make any excuses for blowing it. After reading me the riot act, he grudgingly said I could still come to his house.

I put a bounty of $200 on my stolen car, knowing the people that stole it were desperate for money. I also hoped my dad would help me out as I was flat broke. Sure enough, a couple of nights later someone called. My dad gave me the $200, and we drove out and retrieved my car.

I settled in at my dad's, rising early to read my Bible, a practice I had first started in jail and continued during my times of sobriety. On Sundays, I attended City Church in Kirkland. I tried going to Narcotics Anonymous meetings but quit after only a few. Listening to people recount their drug histories just made me think about how much I wanted to use.

A window cleaning company hired me as a subcontractor and sent me out alone to various job sites, some of which were in areas I used to buy and use crack. It was a perpetual and persistent struggle to stay clean. In the Fall of 2006, five months after moving in with my dad, I relapsed.

Too ashamed and embarrassed to go back home, I stayed out on the streets, surviving by giving people rides, since no one else in the druggie crowd had a driver's license. On Christmas Eve the heater in my station wagon quit working, and I shivered all night in the front seat with only two towels for bedding to cover me. Early Christmas morning, freezing and starving, I drove back to my dad's house, hoping he would give me another chance. He wasn't happy to see me, and I definitely couldn't blame him, but he let me in without saying a word.

23

New Hope International Church

Back in recovery mode again and fighting off the constant cravings, I was thankful to have a roof over my head and food to eat. The cold, wet winter days of 2007 dragged slowly on, and I would take long walks during the day to relieve my restlessness.

On one of my walks, I noticed a small sign that read "New Hope International Church," with an arrow pointing in a direction that I thought had only residential homes. I walked several blocks in that direction and eventually found the church. I asked the people there if it was a Christian, non-denominational church and they told me it was.

The next Sunday I walked to the church to attend service. A rare snowfall had hit Seattle the night before, and the streets were covered in ice. When I got to the church, I was surprised to see an empty parking lot. The door was unlocked, so I went in and sat down alone. About ten minutes later, as I was about to leave, a woman walked in and introduced herself. Her name was Tari. Sitting down next to me, she called someone on her cell phone and discovered the services had been canceled due to the hazardous driving conditions.

Tari and I talked for about half an hour. She told me about her husband, children, work, and most importantly, her faith. I told her about my trials and tribulations. What impacted me most about Tari was that she truly cared about me without judgment, and loved me for who I was.

When I told her about my car needing repairs and I didn't know what it would cost, she took out her checkbook and wrote a check for $175. I refused to accept it. She insisted. When it became apparent to me that the money wasn't as much about me needing it, as it was about her wanting to offer it, I reluctantly accepted the check.

Naturally, I returned for service the following Sunday and was excited to see the unabashed enthusiasm during worship, with everyone's hands raised up to heaven. It was real and wholehearted worship; the kind I had witnessed at the church Mike Knowles had taken me to years earlier on Maui. Back then it had freaked me out, but now I understood; I was all in and loving it!

Yes, I had backslid several times since my jailhouse conversion, but my new found faith had never wavered. Taking my eyes off Jesus never meant that I no longer believed in Him.

24

Connecticut

I sincerely appreciated all the help my dad was giving me, but I was quite lonely living with him and pretty much kept to myself. I would have loved to have hung out with him more, but he just couldn't seem to allow himself to be happy, and that was depressing to be around. My brother once commented, "Dad's only happy when he's unhappy." Funny, sad, but true.

That winter, my High School sweetheart and I reconnected after more than 30 years. She lived alone in a large, upscale home in a gated community in Bellevue, and invited me to live in one of her spare bedrooms. We attended church together, read the Bible together, and I began dreaming that we might even get married and live happily ever after together. But that wasn't meant to be.

It was nice being with someone I could enjoy a pleasant conversation with. A pastor teaching in the New Life Program had once commented that isolation was an abusive relationship, and I agree. I believe all humans are created with an innate desire for companionship. One of the primary reasons addicts relapse is because they feel the rest of the world wants nothing to do with them, even when they are in recovery. The desire to be accepted and be around like-minded people is extremely strong.

Nonetheless, I still managed to mess up once while living with her. My Volvo wagon had broken down again, and I was driving an old banged up car someone from the church we were attending in Kirkland had given me. I sold the Volvo for $300 on Craigslist and then went straight to a dope house. Within hours I had spent all the money, and also gave away the car that was given to me.

Travelers heading East on Interstate 90 at 1am that morning were entertained by a funny sight alongside the highway: pathetic Scott hanging helplessly upside down from an 8 foot chain link fence. While trying to climb over the fence, one of my jean's legs got caught at the top, and I flopped around like a fish on a hook for half an hour before I was finally able to break free.

Exhausted, I spent the next two hours just sitting in the woods, upset at myself for relapsing again. Finally, I managed to stumble back to where I was living, and then just sat on the back porch in my muddy and torn clothes, thoroughly ashamed of myself. My friend let me in when she woke up in the morning and said she had called my dad while searching for me. He told her I wasn't with him, and that they should hope for the best.

After that sorry episode, I managed to avoid any further mishaps while living with her through the winter. In the spring, she sold her house and hired one of my sisters to help me pack and box all of her belongings. We loaded it all into a 28 foot rental truck, and I drove it cross country to a home she owned in Honeoye Falls in upstate New York. Soon after our arrival, I called the golf course in Priest Lake, Idaho and asked if they had any summer job openings. They said yes, and asked if I could start in two weeks. I was thrilled! Priest Lake was always a safe environment for my recovery, and I enjoyed playing golf.

† † †

My youngest son Bryan and his mom were now living in Waterford, Connecticut. Being so close and not seeing him was unacceptable to me, so I called a friend in Maui who owned vacation homes in Connecticut, asking if I could stay in one if I went to visit my son. She told me that would be fine.

I flew to Connecticut. It was important for Bryan to know I was doing my best to spend time with him whenever possible.

25

A Wonderful Summer

From Connecticut, I flew back to my dad's house in Washington State to load my car and head immediately to Priest Lake in northern Idaho, a six-hour drive. Getting away from Seattle as quickly as possible was my best hope of staying clean. My dad asked me where I'd be staying, and I told him I'd figure it out when I got there and not to worry.

I didn't want to ask him if I could stay in the cabin he owned, nor did I want to ask my siblings if I could stay in the cabin they owned, which was right next door to his. There was no sense in trying to make them understand that Priest Lake had always been a safe place for me. I knew they were apprehensive about my staying clean, and understandably so.

So I was really surprised when my dad came outside as I was getting in my car to leave, and gave me the key to his cabin.

The golf course started me out on the grounds crew. Then I got moved into the clubhouse, where one of my duties was tending bar. I never took a drink, didn't even desire one. I knew staying clean at the lake would be easy, and it was, even though wanting the drug I was addicted to never subsided.

I continued to begin every day by reading my Bible, attended Priest Lake Community Church on Sundays, and played a lot of golf, which was free for employees. My sons Kevin and Sean came for two weeks in August, together with my brother's and sisters' families. On my days off I'd join in all the family activities - boating, volleyball, horseshoes, playing board games and cards - all sorts of fun stuff. It was a wonderful summer, a joyful reminder of all the times I had gone to Priest Lake from Maui with my sons before my addiction.

Unfortunately, the golf course job was only seasonal and ended in the Fall. I returned to my dad's house in Seattle and got a job through a temp service to valet cars.

And relapsed.

26

"He's on time"

I bounced around living with other addicts while continuing to work for the valet company. In mid-December, I was put on a crew helping to direct traffic at South Center, Seattle's largest Mall. I felt like such a loser, watching normal people living normal lives, all excited about shopping for gifts and celebrating Christmas with their families. I used to be one of them.

One evening after work the person I was with took me to a church where we could get a free meal. It was called The Cross Discipleship, and when I got there, I discovered they had a live-in Substance Abuse program. I knew I needed to get in that program, but the craving to keep using kept me on the streets.

In desperation, I came up with a plan that would force me to enter the program: If I didn't have a car, I wouldn't be able to work and support my drug habit; so I signed my car over to someone I thought I could trust, with the promise they would give it back when I completed the program in May (just in time to head back to my summer job at the golf course in Priest Lake, Idaho).

I really enjoyed the program at The Cross Discipleship. Bible studies were held every morning and evening. During the day we did chores or went out on work assignments. After two months, we were expected to either have a job or at least be looking for one to pay rent based on our income.

One day, after taking the bus to a job interview, I walked into a convenience store and struck up a conversation with the clerk to talk about Jesus. I asked him what his favorite book in the Bible was and he said Deuteronomy. I asked him why, and he said because that is where the Ten Commandments were. I thought, dang, I can do better than that, so I proceeded to recite Psalm 23.

When I finished, I just stood there with a pompous, self-righteous look on my face, waiting for him to say how wonderful that was. He didn't say anything, just gave me a friendly, compassionate look, as though he genuinely cared about me.

So I continued on, telling him how I wished God had gotten my attention before I had made such a mess out of my life. He then gently spoke three words that I have never forgotten:

"He's on time."

I was instantly convicted. Whereas I knew about God,

this man spoke as though he knew God personally. And his words gave me something I desperately needed - hope.

When I walked into that store, I saw a poor lost soul stuck in a dead end job. When I walked out, I wanted what he had - humility, contentment, peace, and an assurance that God is in control.

27

Divine Intervention

A temp agency sent me to a warehouse, a freezer storage for salmon shipped from Alaska. The temperature was minus 30 degrees inside, and I worked my first day jackhammering ice off the floor. It was brutal, and I quit after only two days. My second job was at a glass recycling plant. All day long, standing outside in the cold Seattle rain, I would take bottles and smash them into smaller pieces so they could be put into a machine and ground into glass sand. My video production days were a distant, haunting memory.

Midway through my fifth month at the Cross Discipleship, I went to the people I had signed my car over to. I told them I'd be completing the program soon and would be needing my car back, as promised. No problem, they told me. But, when the time came for them to sign the car back over to me, they refused. Devastated, I pleaded with them, but to no avail.

And how did I respond to this disappointment? By promptly relapsing.

The next day at the Cross Discipleship, I confessed my relapse and the staff made arrangements for me to go to The Lord's Ranch, a similar ministry, located in Elk, Washington. From there I hoped to find a way to commute to my summer job at Priest Lake Golf Course in Idaho, about a 45-minute drive from Elk. Staying at one of my family's cabins at Priest Lake was no longer an option. After returning from the lake and relapsing the previous summer, my family had made it clear I wasn't even allowed to visit.

† † †

A friend at the Cross Discipleship gave me a ride to the Lord's Ranch. Then someone there shuttled me to and from my job at the golf course. After being there for one week, the owner of the golf course offered to let me stay in a garage across the street from work, and a couple of weeks later my boss' husband sold me his 1989 Toyota truck for $1800 on a bi-monthly payment plan. Now that I had transportation, I could also clean windows as a side job.

As usual, I had no problem staying clean and sober at Priest Lake. And, as usual, when my job ended in the Fall, I returned to Seattle, went straight to the motels and started smoking crack again.

When my money ran out, I scrounged window cleaning jobs by randomly knocking on doors. I'd blow what I made within hours and then sit in my truck all night, waiting for the sun to come up so I could repeat the cycle.

I hated my life.

Early one morning, on a cold and drizzly day in October, after shivering through another sleepless night while sitting in my truck, I recalled what an instructor once said during a Bible study. The Scripture he had referenced was Psalm 23, which talks about the Lord being our Shepherd. He said that when a sheep continuously wandered off, the shepherd would be forced to break one of its legs.

"Break my legs, God. Break my legs," I whispered. I meant it.

That day I got a job right away, which was quite unusual. Usually, I would have to knock on ten to twenty doors before someone would let me clean their windows. It was a three-story house, and the owner asked if I was sure I could reach all the windows. I assured him I could, and offered to clean just the outsides for $180. Before I even started, he handed me two $100 dollar bills. I told him I didn't have change, and he said that was ok.

Five hours later I was on my last set of windows, and to reach high enough I had to place my rickety 20 foot extension ladder on a deck chair the customer had in his backyard, while leaning the top of the ladder against a 3-inch strip of wood dividing two huge plates of glass. Standing on the second step from the top of my ladder and pressing my body against the window to keep from falling backward, I reached as far up as I could with my squeegee.

That's when it happened.

The chair holding my ladder flipped backward, and the top of the ladder slipped off the strip of wood, crashing through the window I was leaning against. With all my weight pressing forward, I should have fallen against the jagged glass and been sliced in two. But, inexplicably, something pulled me backward, and I fell twenty feet to the ground. Landing on my rear end, a leg of the upturned chair struck me on my lower back. Why it didn't go right through me is a mystery.

The owner of the house came running outside and asked if he should call an ambulance. I told him I was having trouble breathing, but that I thought I would be ok. I apologized and offered his money back, but he wouldn't take it.

The next morning, traumatized and knowing something was seriously wrong, I drove to the hospital ER. I couldn't talk, so I wrote on a slip of paper - 'fell from ladder, can't breathe.' They immediately took me in for x-rays, discovered four fractured ribs and a punctured lung, and took me directly into surgery.

God had answered my prayer.

28

Foodbank Prayer

I was in the hospital for eight days. Even though I was probably the latest in a long line of banged-up drug addicts, the staff was incredibly gracious and caring, and made me feel special. I didn't want to leave.

More than anything, I was grateful and relieved that God had answered my prayer. Now, because of my injuries, I would not be able to work and support my drug habit, precisely the result I was praying for. Although penniless and homeless, I felt an inner peace that transcended the uncertainty ahead of me.

† † †

My first stop on the day of my discharge was the nearest library. I felt an urge to share with someone what had happened to me and my current state of affairs. At the library I sent my friend on Maui who owned the Connecticut vacation houses an email. Then, I went to a foodbank.

At the foodbank, they asked if anyone would like prayer to raise their hand. I was the only one who did. A woman then took me into a side room, and I told her about my current situation; that I didn't have a place to live. She prayed for me, and asked me to attend the foodbank's church on Sunday. I promised I would.

Outside, while walking with a bag of food to my truck, my cell phone rang. It was the Maui friend I had emailed from the library. Amazingly, she knew someone who lived in Silverdale, Washington, a town about 75 miles from Seattle, and had called him after receiving my email to see if I could stay with him. He said that would be fine. She told me his name was Charlie and gave me his phone number.

Oh my goodness, I was so happy! I immediately called Charlie. He told me the person living in his spare bedroom had just moved out and that I could come and stay there, rent-free. Wow! I thanked him, told him about my promise to attend the foodbank's church on Sunday, and said I would drive to his place right after the church service ended.

On Sunday at church, I found the woman who had prayed for me at the foodbank and excitedly shared with her how her prayer had been answered immediately. Then, I headed to Silverdale. It was a beautiful drive, but the best view was of the city of Seattle, because it was in my rear view mirror.

It was mid-October, 2008 when I moved into Charlie's. He was awesome. He understood my drug problem and empathized with what I was battling. Charlie worked for a surveying company, and we soon became good friends. I was pretty sore from my accident, so for the first few weeks I just rested, read my Bible and attended church. When I finally started feeling better, I began volunteering at the local foodbank. I also applied at Social Services and qualified for a food card plus $250 monthly cash assistance.

In the first week of January of 2009, I told Charlie I was going to head to San Diego where my youngest son Bryan and his mom were now living. First though I had to go into Seattle to retrieve my set of golf clubs I had pawned.

Sure enough, I relapsed. After two days, I called my brother and asked if he would lend me $80. I told him I just had to get out of Seattle. Thankfully, he gave me $80, and I headed South, knowing the $80 would only get me so far. I didn't care. All that mattered was getting as far away as possible, as fast as possible.

And so began a thirty-two month drug-free odyssey, driving my little 20-year-old pickup all around the country; to anywhere and everywhere but the city of Seattle.

29

Exodus

The biblical book of Exodus chronicles the flight of the Israelites out of Egypt, where they had been enslaved for over 400 years. In the same way, I was now fleeing Seattle, where I had been in bondage to my addiction.

My first stop was Ashland, Oregon, where my son Kevin was attending college. He and I called his mom, and I asked if she would be kind enough to wire me $300 as I was continuing South to be near Bryan. She did, and I was very grateful. Kevin's mom and her husband understood my battle with addiction, and never wavered in helping me.

After spending three days with Kevin, I drove 800 miles further South to where my son Bryan was now living with his mom and grandmother in Escondido, California. Shortly after my arrival, the State of Washington notified me that they would be canceling my food and cash assistance if I stayed in California. As much as I needed the help, going back was not an option. My only concern was staying clean and sober.

I bounced between sleeping on the couch at Bryan's mom's and living in my truck for four months, looking for work but unable to find anything. I called the Priest Lake Golf Course to see if I could work there again for the summer, and was informed that all the positions had already been filled. This was really disheartening news, but I decided to head there anyway, hoping to find any work at all. This would also allow me to attend Kevin's college graduation along the way.

† † †

I had no money and nowhere to live when I finally made it to Priest Lake, but I found some window cleaning jobs, and after living in my truck for two weeks, managed to save enough to rent a room. Before I could, though, Bryan's mom called and asked me to watch Bryan while she went to be with her dad, who was gravely ill, for a few days. I left immediately, even though I knew the 3000-mile round trip drive would wipe out all my savings.

Two weeks later I arrived back at Priest Lake, again without a job, money or a place to live. What I did have was trust in a God who would provide, knowing that I was doing all I could to stay clean and sober. Faithfully, He did. First, it had been Charlie in Silverdale, and now it was Jim and GiGi Horning in Priest Lake, who offered to let me live in their guest cottage rent-free for the entire summer. Then, the local hardware store hired me, even though I didn't know anything about hardware. Praise the Lord!

Restoring my relationship with my family was going to take a little longer, though. Even when my sons Sean and

Kevin stayed at our family cabins that summer, my dad and siblings still wouldn't allow me to come by. I wasn't bitter or resentful. They just didn't understand that when someone was in recovery and doing their best to stay clean and sober, being included in family activities could only help. What good does it do to shun them, other than to cause them to seek companionship with the wrong crowd?

Anyway, there wasn't any sense in worrying about it since there was nothing I could do to change matters. So I just made the most of an awkward situation by joining family gatherings when they would be playing volleyball and pickleball (a game similar to tennis but played with paddles and a whiffle ball) at Hill's Resort.

One evening I bought three humongous porterhouse steaks and invited my sons over to my guest cottage for a bar-b-que. It was the highlight of my summer, just the three of us spending precious moments together. They would be leaving the next day, and I knew I probably wouldn't see them again until the following summer. Sean would be heading back to Maui, and Kevin down to Southern California.

I had no clue where I'd be going.

30

August 2009

Towards the end of August, I gave my boss at the Hardware store my two weeks' notice. I knew that business would drop off substantially after Labor Day. The summer seasonal residents would head South, and the vacation crowds would be gone.

It had been another wonderful, clean and sober summer at the Lake. Oh, there were certainly times when temptation struck, I won't deny that. I would be plagued with crazy thoughts of driving to Seattle just six hours away for a couple of crack-filled days. However, I knew the 'couple' of days would lead to many more days until I was completely broke and on the streets again. As they say in AA - one is too many, a thousand's not enough. And, if I were able to make it back to Priest Lake in time for work, the anguish of keeping a relapse secret, especially from Jim and GiGi, would have haunted me.

God had been showing me that if I stayed on His chosen

path, I would be ok, regardless of my circumstances; if I strayed, His loving discipline awaited. I had developed a reverent fear of the Lord and was desperate to stay clean. It had now been eight months since I had fled Seattle.

This was by far my longest period of sobriety since my addiction started in 2002, not counting the nine months during my second stint in the New Life Program at the Tacoma Rescue Mission.

The previous two summers I had also stayed clean and sober while at the lake, only to relapse shortly after returning to Seattle. So you might wonder – why not just stay at the lake? The answer is simple. With nothing to do there during the winter months, I would go stir crazy! That in itself would drive me straight to the dope house. Also, the winters there are brutally cold, and I don't do cold well. Living on Maui for 27 years will do that to you.

† † †

Throughout my stay at the lake that summer I had been watching and enjoying sermons by Pastor Charles Stanley on the internet. I could tell that they had a large and sophisticated video production department. So I thought perhaps I could get a job at his church in Atlanta, Georgia; even if I couldn't, at least I'd be 2,000 miles away from Seattle.

The only route in and out of Priest Lake is Highway 57. After driving south thirty miles, you arrive at a traffic light and must turn either right or left. In the past, I would always turn right, toward Seattle and the abyss. But this year I was determined to turn left, towards Atlanta and the unknown.

Two days before my planned departure I decided to make a trial run. Seems silly, I know. Only suffering addicts trying to maintain their sobriety can relate to the internal struggle and anxiety I was experiencing. Anyway, I drove the thirty miles south on Highway 57 to the town of Priest River and closed my bank account. Now I had $1700 cash in my pocket, a scary thing for an addict struggling to stay clean. Then I headed East, planning to reach Kalispell, Montana in time to turn around and make it back to Priest Lake before dark.

It was a longer drive than anticipated, so I had to turn around before reaching Kalispell. While cruising along and enjoying the spectacular scenery, thoughts and visions of smoking crack suddenly began to bombard my senses. I knew it was demonic, and I started praying up a storm, but the onslaught only intensified. I tried everything I could to push it out of my mind – to no avail. I had never experienced cravings this intense, this unrelenting. Thinking back on it now, it usually didn't take much to entice me to relapse, so the temptations never had to escalate. But now, more determined than ever to stay clean, the thoughts were literally screaming at me!

Finally, I yelled, "You win!" and gave up. I was a drug addict, and I had no choice but to do what drug addicts do.

Instantly, the thoughts disappeared! It was like listening to the worst music in the world, getting louder and louder, and then, suddenly, it stops; total silence - except for the steady hum of my little truck's motor.

The remaining two hours of the trip were a fog. I stumbled into my cabin and collapsed on the bed; physically/mentally/spiritually defeated. I woke up the next morning looking for anything to keep myself from reliving the drama I had experienced the day before.

Outside my cabin was a huge pile of firewood that Jim and I had cut, split and hauled during the summer. I spent the entire day stacking it into a shed. It was back-breaking work, and just what I needed because at the end of the day I was too tired to pack my truck. In all of my travels, I had always packed everything the night before and headed out between 4 – 5am. This time I wasn't in my normal rush to get to the dope house mode, and hoped a change in my usual departure routine would help me in my battle to stay clean. The next morning I took my time meticulously cleaning Jim and Gigi's guest cabin. Then I slowly packed all my worldly possessions and loaded my truck.

Before the trial run, I had a false sense of security, believing that the eight months of staying clean on my own without the structured environment of a treatment program would be enough for me to make the proper turn when I reached the light. But the drive to Kalispell had dispelled that false security. The moment that I had surrendered to those overpowering voices was still fresh in my mind, and that scared me. What would happen today? One thing was for sure - it wasn't going to be as easy as I had thought, and just knowing that was huge.

The trial run had served a purpose after all. It alerted me to expect a battle. The Bible tells us that the flesh desires what is contrary to the spirit, and the spirit what is contrary to the flesh. My flesh wanted to go west; my spirit wanted to go anywhere but west. I got in my truck and headed south on Highway 57. At the light, I calmly turned left. Within 10 miles I pulled off to the side of the road. My mind was racing. It wasn't that I feared heading into the unknown, but my addiction was raging. It was literally screaming at me, "What are you doing?!"

I jumped out and leaned against my truck, breathed in the fresh mountain air and took in the beautiful scenery to calm myself. The voice of addiction was reminding me that the farther I went in this direction, the longer it would take me to get to Seattle when I turned around - not if, but when I turned around.

I walked over and stood gazing upon the gently flowing Pend Oreille River. In a daze, I slowly got back into my truck, turned around, and headed back west, toward Seattle. At the light where I had taken the left turn, I pulled into a gas station and bought a pack of cigarettes. I had struggled throughout the summer to quit smoking, but now I didn't care - my cravings would soon be fed in Seattle, followed by the usual misery and regret.

The first thing I saw the next morning was the sun rising beyond the majestic Grand Teton Mountains. I had turned back around! I groggily recollected that I had driven as far as I could until I was too tired to continue, and then had pulled off at a rest stop somewhere in Wyoming and fallen asleep in the driver's seat of my truck.

It wasn't so much the thought of being broke, homeless and starting all over for the umpteenth time that had got me turned back around. Heck, addiction doesn't care about any of that. It was by the grace of God that I was on this path. He gets ALL the glory! I knew that it wasn't me at all. He had mercy on me and strengthened me, and I was fully aware of His presence. I knew no matter what hardships were sure to come, nothing mattered other than doing what was right in His eyes. He would take care of the rest.

This is not to say that the internal struggle went away. Every 60 miles I would get a thought, "If you turn around now, you can get to Seattle in 6 hours, 7 hours, 8 hours…".

When I reached 1000 miles from Seattle, the temptations only changed to "Not to worry, you can find that stuff in Atlanta." Crazy! Of course, I had no intention of doing that, but the thoughts persisted anyway.

That's addiction.

31

Atlanta

It took me four days to reach the outskirts of Atlanta. Along the way, I always slept in my truck at rest stops. Motels, at least the ones I could afford, scared me. I had spent too much time in them doing drugs to feel comfortable. Plus, I needed to conserve my finances. I hoped that Charles Stanley's church would have a network that could help me find inexpensive housing in a Christian environment, and also help me to find a job.

The week before leaving Priest Lake, I had gone to the library and printed Mapquest directions to his church. I had also researched the Sunday service times. So now I just hunkered down in my vehicle at a truck stop about 25 miles west of Atlanta and waited until Sunday rolled around. It was kind of a miserable existence; the early September humidity was stifling. Yet I was completely at peace, reading my Bible and looking forward to whatever God had already prepared for me.

Early Sunday morning I headed out in a torrential rainstorm toward the city. I was driving in the far right lane of a four-lane highway, when out of nowhere a car came hydroplaning sideways across all four lanes right in front of me, flew off the road and flipped several times end over end. I pulled over to the shoulder of the highway and ran toward it not expecting any survivors as the car was totally destroyed. Amazingly, by the time I got to it, the only occupant was climbing out a broken back window with just a small scratch on his head. I couldn't believe it. It was a miracle.

At that moment I couldn't help but think of the encounter I had years earlier with my son Sean about my drug use when he asked me, "Why can't you just stop?" and I responded, "I wish I could." When that guy's car was hydroplaning, I'm sure he wished he could stop too. But he couldn't. Although the car was a total loss, as was most everything in my life, God had kept us both alive.

I looked, and probably smelled, like a drowned rat by the time I finally made it to Charles Stanley's church. Everyone else there was dressed in their Sunday best. Church attire is much more casual in the Northwest, so I kind of stood out in the crowd, but I didn't mind. I was just thrilled to be there. After viewing Charles Stanley's sermons countless times on the internet, it was surreal to see him live. When the service ended I got the contact info for the person coordinating the media crews and then went to one of the breakout meetings to meet people. It was a start.

In the middle of the following week, still living in my truck, I decided it would be a good idea to drive to the church and ask about potential housing and fill out a job application for any openings in the video department. First though, I rented a room in a sleazy motel next to the truck stop so I could take a shower. I knew it would give me the jitters, and it did. Not surprisingly, I could tell the people in the other rooms were up to no good.

I was able to make it to the church unscathed and asked the receptionist if I could see someone who might be able to give me some advice. The receptionist spoke with someone on the phone and informed me that a pastor would come out and meet with me shortly. What transpired next totally threw me off course.

A James Bond clone came out, dressed in a tailored suit, and introduced himself as Pastor So and So and asked, "What can I do for you?"

"Well, I drove down here from northern Idaho because I enjoyed watching Charles Stanley's sermons on the internet. I don't know anybody, never been to this part of the country. I was hoping you might have a network or ministry that could help me find a room to rent in a Christian living situation."

"We don't give out money."

Huh? I hadn't asked for any money. But, more than what he said, was the condescending tone in how he said it. I thought to myself, if anyone interested in being a Christian ever met this guy, they would definitely run the other way. Fortunately, my faith was rock solid, and his attitude wasn't going to shake it or my opinion of Charles Stanley. However, I did determine then and there that I definitely didn't want to be associated with this church at all.

He said a prayer, and the meeting was over.

You might think I was a bit frazzled at this turn of events;

I wasn't. In my heart, I knew God was using this meeting to move me onward. If I had been up to no good, I would have been frightened, but that wasn't the case here. I knew I just needed to wait on the Lord and He would lead me where He wanted me to be. I just hoped that it would be soon.

It was. I walked out to my car and called my friend Yvette in Maui. I just needed to talk with someone who was familiar with my struggles and cared about me. She said I could go up to Connecticut, stay in her vacation houses and earn money painting and doing yard work. This would also enable me to spend time with my son Bryan. He and his mom had moved from California back to Connecticut during the summer.

This was perfect!

32

I am His

The temptations that had plagued me during my drive to Atlanta subsided significantly on the 1000 mile journey north to Connecticut, but they were still present nonetheless, and always would be.

Yvette's three vacation rental homes were located in two quaint little coastal towns; one in Guilford and the other two in Old Saybrook. My initial room would be in what Yvette called 'the shack in the back.' And that's exactly what it was, a shack, situated right behind the larger of her two rentals in Old Saybrook. That was fine with me. Amazing how any place with a roof and a bed can seem like a palace after living in a vehicle. Her three houses were rented to vacationers, but I was allowed to stay in them when they weren't rented. So and for the next two months I bounced between the houses and the shack.

My first priority was to find a church I felt most comfortable as most in this part of the country are affiliated with specific religious denominations – Methodist, Episcopalian, Lutheran, etc. Therefore I went to the library and found three that were non-denominational churches. I attended each one, then made my choice.

I visited with my son Bryan in Waterford whenever possible as well as Sean's mom in Branford. I spent most of my time working around Yvette's properties, for which Yvette paid me an hourly wage. Her son Chris, who lived nearby in New London, helped his mom manage the vacation houses, and we became good friends.

One day, as I was sharing my life story with him, he looked at me and asked, "So, if you were with someone, and they started using that stuff right in front of you, what would you do?"

After thinking for a moment, to give myself a chance to respond honestly, I replied, "I wouldn't be able to refuse it. That's why I am doing everything I can to avoid being in that type of situation."

Recovery is a daily grind, especially when you're living in survival mode. I wasn't craving it, but the temptation to artificially escape my nomadic existence by getting high was always present. The occasional 'drug' dreams also haunted me. This is a phenomenon that afflicts all recovering addicts, though it does lessen over time. After using in my sleep, it was always a relief to wake up knowing it was only a dream. However, I would be totally disappointed in myself that I had relapsed – even though it had only been in a dream.

Would the day ever come when, in a dream, I'd turn it down? I hoped so. I really, really hoped so.

My original plan when I arrived in Connecticut was to drive back to Priest Lake in the Spring, but as winter approached, the thought of being cooped up all alone in the shack when all the houses were rented was depressing. The only other option available was a friend I had met at church in Priest Lake. His name was Gordon, and he told me I could stay in his spare bedroom if I ever needed a place. Gordon's neighbors said he just sat alone in his cabin during the winters. I felt sorry for him. Once I had completed all of Yvette's work projects, I piddled around for a couple days. Finally, I called Gordon and asked about coming to his cabin. He said that would be fine.

Was this the right decision though? Or was I just tired of flying by the seat of my pants, hoping a change of venue would create a change in my fortunes? I had an assurance in my spirit that it was God's will to come East. I didn't have that same assurance now as I packed my truck to go back.

Around 7pm I went to my room, set the alarm for 4am and fell asleep, feeling like the homeless people you see pushing their shopping carts full of their worldly possessions around town. The only difference being me and them was I had a truck and was driving my worldly possessions around the country.

I was awakened out of a deep sleep by someone knocking on my door.

"Whaaaaaaaat?" I groaned.

"There's someone here I want you to meet," Yvette said through the door.

"I'm in bed."

"You need to come out and meet her. She's a Christian."

Yvette knew about my faith, something I didn't have when

we knew each other on Maui, but she didn't share many of my beliefs, and I sincerely doubted she could tell the difference between a genuine Christian and a snowman.

"Yvette, I've got a long drive tomorrow. Just let me sleep" I protested.

We were still talking through the door. Normally I would have initiated the conversation by inviting her to come in, but I wasn't in a normal mood.

"No, really" she responded, knowing that I doubted her 'she's a Christian' assessment.

"Not going to happen," I grumbled.

"You have to come out and meet her. You have to!" She persisted.

Ugh! I crawled out of bed, shuffled into the living room and fell into a sofa chair. Yvette introduced me to her friend Pamela. Then they immediately resumed talking about medical issues, a topic I was thoroughly disinterested in. In fact, the only thing that interested me was going back to bed. After slouching half asleep in my chair for about 15 minutes, I stood up, turned to Pamela, and apologized.

"It was nice meeting you. Sorry I wasn't more sociable. I've got a long drive ahead of me tomorrow and I just need to get some sleep." Then, I turned around and went back to bed.

It wasn't long before Yvette was knocking on my door again.

"Scott, Pamela might have a place for you to stay so you can be near your son. She told me to have you call her in the morning if you're interested. You should check it out."

"Ok," I replied.

I didn't know what else to say. Where did this come from? I thought that the first impression I had given Pamela was borderline rude. When I called her in the morning, she explained she owned a building she referred to as 'the Barn' in Clinton. Two ladies were living in it, and she said they would feel safer if a man lived there with them, and that I could also help take care of the property.

I'm thinking 'The Barn'? The visual of a dilapidated structure came to my mind. But, Clinton was on my planned route, so I told her I'd check it out. If I didn't like what I saw, I could just keep on trucking west.

Pamela also told me that she would not have stopped at the house last night if she had known Yvette was in town. They had a falling out some time ago. The only reason she had knocked on the door was that she had seen the light on and thought maybe Chris was there. But when Yvette answered the door, they immediately patched up their differences and began talking again.

Was God intervening in my travel plans? If so, there was no doubt in my mind that it was He who prompted Pamela to come by the night before my planned departure.

Thoughts of pigeon poop dropping on me as I slept in hay next to a cow instantly evaporated when I arrived at 'the Barn.' Although the building was shaped like a barn, it was anything but that. The bottom floor was a huge shop area. The second floor consisted of two large storage rooms, a full bath, and two furnished rooms with separate entrances off the hallway. One of the women lived in one of these rooms. The other would be mine. Upstairs on the third floor was a large one-bedroom apartment occupied by the other woman.

The property was located in a rural area. A single home was on each side, behind was a river and in front was a lawn bordered by a white picket fence. The public library was only two blocks away, walking distance. This was a major plus. I loved spending time in libraries, and would utilize their computer to do my emailing.

I drove back to Old Saybrook, called Pamela, and told her it all looked good to me if it was good for her. She then told me I would have to meet with her husband before a decision could be made, and that he would call me to set up a time and place. Later that day he called and asked if I could meet him at a convenience store in Old Saybrook. I noted a definite tone of skepticism in his voice, like this was going to be a complete waste of his time. I told him I'd be there in a small black Toyota truck.

As I stood next to my truck waiting, I pondered this series of events and thanked God for taking upon Himself the decision of whether I was to leave or stay. I finally felt at peace. The uncertainty I had felt about my decision to go to Gordon's for the winter was now replaced by an assurance that God was in control.

A white Ford F150 rumbled up next to me and a man got out.

"Are you Scott?"

"I am."

"I'm DJ."

He leaned back against his truck, folded his arms across his chest and asked, "So, what's your story?"

The way he said it made it sound more like an interrogation than a simple question, yet I couldn't have been more at ease. I wasn't concerned about making a good impression, only an honest one. I knew that the final decision wasn't his to make. And I knew the One that would make it. I told him my story and ended with suggesting he could contact Yvette as a reference.

"I hate Yvette" DJ spat.

"If God wants me to stay, that's fine. If not, that's fine as well. He's in control," I said calmly.

"What was the drug?"

"Crack.

"How long have you been clean?"

"Since January – 11 months."

"How much money do you have?"

"$900."

"We'll pray about it."

"Ok."

And with that, DJ got in his truck and drove off. I laughed all the way back to Yvette's. She was my only reference, and DJ hated her. Too funny!

The next morning Pamela called me. "Scott, DJ and I prayed about it last night, and this morning God spoke three words to me, "He is Mine.""

† † †

I thanked God as I moved into my room at the Barn. What He had said to Pamela didn't surprise me. When I had asked Jesus Christ to be my Lord and Savior, my spirit had been born again into God's family. I knew I was a child of God. I knew that I belonged to Him, but that He had said it so clearly to them was awesome! His declaration was personal, and I am humbled whenever I think about it.

I am His. What a blessed assurance!

33

The Barn and Beyond

The barn was a literal Godsend. Not only did I have a nicely furnished room, but I was also given work to do in exchange for rent, mainly grounds keeping. When the snow fell, I used their truck with a plow attached to clear the driveway and the parking lot across the street.

DJ was transferred to Sugar Land, Texas that winter. Pamela had health issues and had two young children to care for, so I regularly went to their home in Old Saybrook to help out. In the Spring, they purchased a home in Texas, and I helped load and then drove the moving truck for them. It was a three-day journey each way, which I made twice to transport everything. We turned the truck into the rental agency in Texas after my second trip, and I flew back to Connecticut. Then I began the 2700 mile drive back cross country to Priest Lake, Idaho for the summer.

By the time I reached Chicago my truck's warning indicators were lighting up like a Christmas tree. My funds were meager and I was praying up a storm that it wouldn't conk out. The the next day, giving God another opportunity to reveal Himself to me in more amazing ways, it broke down.

I limped off the highway on an exit ramp somewhere in Wisconsin and rolled to a stop. By the time I got out I was amazed to see that three cars had stopped to help me. I just looked at them for a moment, speechless, feeling God's presence in my time of need. We hooked my jumper cables up to one of their cars, charging my battery enough to get me into the nearest town. An attendant at an auto parts store checked it out, told me I needed a new alternator, and gave me directions to a shop that could install it.

I was down to just enough money to cover my gas for the remainder of the trip, so I called Gordon at the lake. He was kind enough to pay for the part and repair estimate with his credit card – a little over $200. They didn't know when the repairs would be finished, so I decided to walk over to a nearby mall to sit and wait.

My phone rang.

It was Pamela. She asked where I was. I said somewhere in the middle of nowhere. She said she wanted to use her credit card to get me a room for the night. I thanked her but said I just wanted to keep driving. She then told me God had specifically told her to call me and get me a room, so I finally relented. I asked someone the name of the town and called her back. A few minutes later, she called to let me know she had booked a room in my name at a nearby Holiday Inn.

It was late in the afternoon when I finally saw the mechanic pull my truck out of their garage. I walked over, paid with Gordon's credit card info and went out to leave. When I started the truck, it made a weird clanking sound, and I heard something hit the pavement. I got out, looked under underneath, and saw a large bolt on the ground. When I showed it to the mechanic, he denied responsibility.

Fortunately, his boss overruled him and agreed to fix the problem, but said it would take some time and the shop was already closed for the day. He asked if I had a place to stay.

"Yes," I smiled, "Yes, I do."

Once again, God had gone before me and prepared the way. I was in heaven, knowing it was heaven sent; a room, a shower, and a bed. Best of all of course was how it had happened, reaffirming my faith in knowing that God would never leave me nor forsake me.

Someone going through a tough time had once complained to me that God wasn't coming through with His promise to never give us more than we can handle. I haven't read that verse in the Bible. But that's precisely what He does - push us to our limits so we can have the opportunity to trust Him and experience His deliverance.

The well-known story "Footprints" by Margaret Fish is a beautiful illustration of this. In it, someone is talking to God about two sets of footprints on a beach, representing our walk with God through life. During the toughest times, however, there was only one set of footprints.

"Why were you not walking with me when I needed you most, God?" the person in the story inquires.

"I was with you," God responded. "Those were my footprints, and it was during those times when you needed me most that I was carrying you."

So beautiful, and so true!

The next day a different repairman picked me up at 11am and gave me a ride back to the repair shop. I started my truck, no bolts clanged to the pavement, and I headed west. As I drove, it was comforting to know I had a place to stay when I got there. Considering the fact that I had been clean and sober for 17 months, I hoped my family would welcome me back into the fold as well.

It was late May when I arrived, too late to apply for the summer seasonal jobs. The only income I could generate was cleaning a few windows here and there. My goal was to earn enough money to cover my gas expense to get to wherever I would be driving after the summer ended. I volunteered at the local foodbank, and a woman there helped me get on food stamps.

The thoughts that had tormented me the previous summer of racing over to Seattle for a few days had subsided significantly, but not entirely. Physical cravings were no longer an issue, but the drug dreams persisted, and I was still relapsing in every one. When awake, my main struggle was with boredom and loneliness. These feelings I knew could trigger a relapse, so I tried to stay busy.

Each morning after my coffee and Bible reading, I would walk two miles to Hills Resort and get the newspaper, then walk back and read it on Gordon's dock. Once a week I would drive Gordon 75 miles to do his shopping in Spokane. I mowed and weed whacked the grounds at Priest Lake Community Church every two weeks. I'd go to the driving range and putting green at the golf course. And of course, I'd spend time at the local library, using their computers and checking out books.

Most importantly, I stayed clean and sober – one day at a time. I had lots of friends at the lake; people who were genuinely happy to see me. I'd bump into them at church, the store, the golf course, Hill's Resort, wherever. In fact, I'd go sit on the tailgate of my truck outside the laundromat just because I knew someone familiar would stop by and we could share some small talk, a laugh, a hug, a handshake.

† † †

My family's cabins were only a five-minute walk from Gordon's, but I resisted the urge to go there, fearing rejection. Then one day my brother walked over to Gordon's and invited me to come and hang out at their dock. It was like old times. My dad stayed on the beach, sitting and talking with my niece who was drinking a beer. I noticed he didn't seem to mind her drinking even though he knew that she had her own substance abuse issues.

Soon after I returned to Gordon's, my brother called to let me know our dad told him to tell me I couldn't come back. My brother was genuinely sorry, but I told him not to worry. Dad's attitude didn't surprise me nor did I allow it to upset me. All my bitterness towards him had left with that 28-page letter of reconciliation I had mailed from jail a few years earlier. The power of forgiveness had set me free from the bondage of unforgiveness, forever.

I was happy that my relationship with my siblings was being slowly restored. When my sons Kevin and Sean arrived for two weeks in late July we all had a wonderful time, getting together every day at Hill's Resort. When my sons left, I was ready to go as well, knowing it wouldn't be the same without them.

But where would I go?

As usual, God intervened on my behalf.

34

San Diego

Shortly after my sons' departure from the lake, Bryan's mom called and asked if I would drive her SUV to San Diego. She told me Bryan was being bullied at his school in Connecticut and she wanted to take him back to the High School he had attended near San Diego as a freshman. She had a two bedroom apartment lined up there and said I could sleep on the living room couch until her mom came out to join them. I emailed the church where I had volunteered when I was in that area the first time, and they offered me an $8/hr position in their media department.

I drove to San Diego from Priest Lake, parked my truck, and flew to Connecticut. The day after I arrived in Connecticut, we packed their SUV as much as we could possibly get into it. When we were done, I barely had enough room to get into the driver's seat. Then it was off to San Diego, a 3000-mile drive. Bryan and his mom took an airplane.

One evening, while doing some work at the church, a man from the Maintenance Department walked up to me and asked where I lived. Without missing a beat, I asked him where he needed a ride to. He said Oceanside, which was about a 20-minute drive beyond where I was staying. I said I'd be happy to give him a ride, and refused the gas money he offered.

His name was Jimmy Chaidez, and we became close friends. Jimmy didn't have a license and had to take a bus, a train, then another bus just to get to and from his job at the church. I told him I would be his transportation. He lived with his wife and four sons, and offered to rent me a room in their house for only $200 a month, which I readily accepted.

My days were busy. I had a full-time job, gave Jimmy rides to work, helped get Bryan to and from school, and played pickleball two or three times a week for recreation. Life was going well.

Then I got hurt.

I blew my knee out at church moving a stage prop, and an MRI revealed that I had a torn meniscus. The head pastor suggested I apply for Workmen's Compensation. I did, but soon learned it's a process that takes months to reconcile.

I could no longer help with staging, and this didn't go over well with my supervisor. He reduced my work to videotaping a one hour Bible study on Wednesday evenings, a one-hour church service on Saturdays, and four hours on Sundays. My commute was 50 miles round trip in heavy traffic, hardly worth it, considering that I would now be making less than $50 a week, of which Bryan's child support took half.

I was again in dire financial straits, and I couldn't play pickleball. I became severely depressed. The wilderness wandering and survivor mode was taking a toll, and I wondered if it would ever end. One evening I half-heartedly went to a seedy part of San Diego looking for crack, but managed to turn around without ever getting out of my car. I did, however, go to a bar a few nights later and got drunk on beer, my first alcohol in over two years. I was slipping, and I knew I had to get away.

First though, I had to complete ten sessions of physical therapy, in order to qualify for Workman's Compensation, and this would take four weeks. I decided that when it was over, I would drive up to Priest Lake, always a safe place for me to stay clean and sober. I notified my supervisor at the church about my departure in one month and began training someone to operate the video system. By the time I finished in April, my finances had dwindled to almost nothing, and my knee was still in bad shape. Making matters worse, the physical therapist tried to say my knee was ok. This was most likely to appease the insurance company, but my case was far from being resolved. I left for Priest Lake.

† † †

Gordon had sold his cabin and was now living in a warehouse on property he owned at the lake. He said I could live in a trailer he had there rent-free, and offered to pay me $12 an hour to work around the property.

Gordon's trailer was NICE! It had a bedroom with a queen size bed, living room, dining area, full kitchen, and best of all - lots of windows (I love natural light). The room I had lived in at Jimmie's house had no windows, which only added to my despair. I was super happy, and looked forward to an enjoyable summer in peaceful Priest Lake, Idaho.

My first project was to organize Gordon's warehouse garage and storage container. That took two weeks. Then it was on to grubbing his property, which kept me busy for most of the summer. I enjoyed the work and, of course, the income.

I also drove Gordon on his weekly shopping excursions down to Spokane, until one day he insisted on doing the driving. He could be ornery at times. I told him he could do as he wanted, but I wasn't going with him if he drove because I didn't feel safe. So off he went. That night, at around 1am, my phone rang. I had a feeling what it was going to be about. Sure enough, it was the emergency room down in Priest River. They said Gordon was alright, but his truck was totaled. I drove down and fetched him. He complained that the oncoming driver was flashing his headlights. I told him that was because he was driving in the oncoming driver's lane.

There was no doubt in my mind that Gordon's driving days were over. He was 80 years old and had totaled two trucks within the last year. But, he insisted on getting another vehicle, so I took him to the dealership. I told the sales people there was no way I would ride along with them on the test drives and warned they might want to make it short. The look of pure terror on their faces when they returned was priceless! He finally bought a used Jeep Grand Cherokee with all the bells and whistles. The sales guy gave him the keys, and gave me a look that said 'good luck to him making the 75-mile drive back to the lake in one piece.' I followed him in my truck, praying all the way as he swerved back and forth in front of me.

The best news that summer was finally being allowed to visit and spend my leisure time with my family at their cabins. All three of my sons, Bryan, Kevin, and Sean came and stayed at the cabins for two weeks in August, and they were happy their dad was no longer being treated as an outcast. So was I.

When my sons left, I began to wonder, as usual, where I would go when the summer ended. And, as always, God provided. On a hunch, I gave Charlie a call. We had kept in contact since the time he had taken me in at Silverdale, after my ladder accident. I knew he was now doing survey work in North Dakota, and I told him I was available if he needed any help. He said he'd let me know.

Less than a week later, Charlie called back and asked me how soon I could get to North Dakota. His assistant had disappeared with his work vehicle for two days, so he fired him and sent him back to Washington State.

I told Charlie I'd head out immediately.

35

North Dakota

It was around noon when Charlie had called, and I was excited to pack my truck, clean the trailer, say goodbye to Gordon and begin the thousand-mile drive east to Williston, North Dakota. Charlie needed someone right away, and I was determined to be there for him, just as he had been there for me.

The drive through Williston the next day was an eye-opener. It was the epicenter of an oil boom hitting that part of the country, and there were more 18-wheelers on the road than cars and trucks. My little Toyota did have one thing in common with the locals - a cracked windshield.

I rendezvoused with Charlie in what seemed like the middle of nowhere and followed him to where he was living in a dilapidated Winnebago parked on private property. Just like the people on Maui had been renting tent space on their properties in 1976, here people were renting space on their properties to park mobile homes and trailers. Thousands of people were flooding the area for work, overwhelming the housing market; some were paying up to $1000/week for a motel room that would typically cost $150/week.

I had been on the job for only a week when Charlie announced we would be driving his SUV to Silverdale so that he could meet up with his girlfriend and fly with her to San Diego for a few days vacation. It took us two days to make the 1300 mile drive, and the day after we arrived, I drove Charlie and his girlfriend to Seattle, dropped them off at SeaTac airport … and relapsed.

Seattle's scourge had struck swiftly.

For two years and eight months I had traveled around the country, avoiding the one area I was prone to relapse, and had managed to stay clean. And now I had blown it. But blaming Seattle was a pointless excuse. It was time to pick up the pieces again, and it wasn't going to be easy, but with every ounce of willpower I could muster I forced myself to quit and drive back to Silverdale after just one night. A great sense of guilt weighed me down, and I was determined to confess my relapse to Charlie when he returned in a few days.

In the meantime, I kept struggling with the temptation to go back out. The cravings were again insatiable. My mind was pleading with me to go back before I lost the opportunity, and argued that I had already blown it anyway. Being all by myself didn't help matters either, but the overriding factor that kept me at the house was Charlie's car. He had entrusted it to me. SeaTac airport was only a few blocks from where I had gone and used. Silverdale was sixty miles. I was desperately reaching for anything that would tip the scales in favor of not going back, and his car did just that.

I managed to stay put; that's the good news. The bad news was that I chickened out on telling Charlie about my relapse. I didn't want him to monitor my future opportunities to use. Not that I was planning on using again, but then I hadn't planned on relapsing when I took them to the airport. At least I didn't think I did. Addiction is brutally deceptive and opportunistic.

Five days later I picked Charlie and his girlfriend up at SeaTac airport. A a couple days after that, he and I drove the 1300 miles back to our spot in North Dakota. Then, it was back to work.

† † †

The first week of October, Charlie decided to fly back to the East Coast for a week and visit family. He told me to drive my truck back to Silverdale while he was gone. The plan was for me to hang out at his house for a few days and then take the Amtrak train back to North Dakota. This way, when we broke camp for the winter and went to his home in Silverdale, I could drive his SUV, and he would drive the Winnebago.

Back near Seattle, lots of money in my pocket, my own vehicle, a recent relapse, and no accountability?

This was a recipe for disaster.

36

The Final Meltdown

The cravings intensified with each mile. I drove in a daze, not wanting to give in to them, but not fighting them either. It was all I could do to drive past Seattle and continue on to Silverdale. I parked my truck at Charlie's house, went inside and made something to eat. I should have been dog tired after driving 1300 miles but my heart was racing. I got in bed, rolled up in the fetal position and pulled the covers over my head. After only ten minutes or so, I threw the covers off, stuffed just enough money to last one day in my pocket, and headed out to Seattle.

As planned, I was out of the money I had taken with me by the next day. As planned, this forced me to return to Silverdale. What didn't go according to plan was staying in Silverdale, and not going out again. I ran into the house, grabbed just enough money to last one more day, and raced back to Seattle.

I was in full blown relapse mode. Coming down off that

stuff is the worst feeling in the world. At this point, it was not about enjoying a high, it was all about self-medication. Each time I used, my tolerance kept increasing, so it took more to get high. And the more I used, the more I progressed from a state of euphoria to an insane state of delusional paranoia.

On my fourth trip, I remember sitting in a motel room, loading up my pipe, and saying in a hushed voice to myself: "Maybe, if I'm lucky, on this hit my heart will explode."

Another person in the room heard me.

"What did you say?"

"You heard me" I replied quietly.

I had lost my will to live, having smoked enough crack the past four days to kill an elephant. In my mind, it wouldn't be suicide. No, this would be accidental. My life wasn't worth living anymore. The world would be a better place without me.

I was scared, but somehow I didn't die, and headed back to Silverdale. On my way out of the motel parking lot, two strangers approached me and gave me two BB sized bags and said I could pay them when I returned later to buy some more. This was weird, dealers don't do that. They gave me their room number, and I drove off, putting one of the tiny bags in my pocket and the other under the seat.

I never did return to the motels, nor did I even use the drugs they gave me. Better yet, all praise be to God, this was over seven years ago, I've been clean and sober ever since, and always will be.

The date was October 7, 2011.

37

Bangor Nuclear Submarine Base

I was so totally caught up in my addiction I thought there was little, more likely zero, chance that I would be on that train back to North Dakota. It was about 10 in the morning, broad daylight, as I drove south on Interstate 5 to Tacoma. I took an exit, and then headed west toward Silverdale, crossing over the Narrows Bridge. The last thing I remember was passing the exit to Gig Harbor, then nothing, then a snapshot of me going straight toward the wide sloping ditch separating my lanes from the oncoming traffic, then nothing, then – Bam! Bam! Bam!

My eyes opened slowly in a bleary haze as I tried focusing on what looked like men in military uniforms, some armed with M16 rifles, surrounding my truck. One of them was banging on the driver's side window. As I rolled down the window, he ordered me to get out of my truck. Dazed and confused, I did as I was told.

"What are you doing here?" He demanded brusquely.

"Doing where?" I mumbled.

"Don't you know where you are?"

I looked around. My truck was parked up against a fence with razor wire in a wooded area. Where was I?

"I have no idea where I am, or how I got here," I stammered, "The last thing I remember is driving on the highway toward where I live in Silverdale."

"This is Bangor Nuclear Submarine Base," he said sternly, "You're trespassing on federally restricted land."

I grimaced at the irony. About 10 years earlier I had done a video shoot for the Navy in Pearl Harbor, riding a PT boat and shooting landmarks to help subs navigate. From that job I got hired to do the same here at Bangor a few months later, riding a PT boat in Puget Sound, shooting a building here, a cliff there, whatever they pointed out.

Now I was back at Bangor, in handcuffs, a strung-out drug addict.

But how I had ended up here this time was a real mystery. I had blacked out behind the wheel of my truck, going 60 miles an hour on the highway near Gig Harbor, a town 28 miles south of where I was headed to my home in Silverdale. Bangor is another 6 miles further beyond Silverdale.

As they searched my truck, a medic ran some tests on me to see if I was fit to drive. They found the tiny bag I had hidden under my seat and asked me what it was. I told them it was cocaine. They put me in one of their vehicles, and huddled up to decide what to do with me. I overheard their leader say he was going to give me a stern lecture and let me go.

They were about to send me on my way when, suddenly,

the Kitsap county sheriff arrived on the scene. He put me in his set of handcuffs and hauled me off to jail, telling me along the way that I would be charged with felony possession of a controlled substance. As bad as that sounded, what grieved me the most was letting Charlie down. We had several surveying jobs left to complete, and he was also counting on me to drive his SUV back to Silverdale when we wrapped up.

After being processed at the police station, I was told I would be arraigned first thing in the morning. I called Charlie to let him know what I had gotten myself into. He was super nice, yet understandably concerned about my not being able to get back to North Dakota. I told him I'd call right after court.

The next morning I cringed as the judge threw the book at everyone that went before me. Then it was my turn. Unbelievably, the prosecutor recommended releasing me on my own recognizance! I was the only one there that didn't get sent back to his jail cell. Outside the jail, I called Charlie with the fantastic news, and the following day I was on a train back to North Dakota. I received more good news a couple days later when my Public Defender called and said he had raised an issue regarding the search of my truck, and asked me if I would be willing to plead to a misdemeanor paraphernalia charge. I said, 'Absolutely!'

There is no doubt in my mind that God had taken the wheel of my truck when I blacked out. In fact, I knew He had saved my life on numerous occasions, and yet I had continued to backslide. I just couldn't understand why He had not given up on me.

A few weeks later, on November 13, 2011, God Himself would tell me why.

38

"I love you, Scott. I love you, Scott"

Charlie and I wrapped up our North Dakota surveying jobs in early November and returned to his home in Silverdale. The plan was to live there through the winter, surveying throughout Western Washington, and then go back to North Dakota in the spring.

On the first Sunday after our arrival, November 13, 2011, I drove 75 miles to New Hope International Church. As I got out of my truck in the parking lot, I could hear the music playing and the people singing inside. I started crying. When someone cheerfully greeted me at the door, I could only respond with a nod, not bothering to wipe away the tears now streaming down my cheeks.

Years earlier I had cried in the back seat of a car, because I felt sorry for myself. This was different. Now I was, simply, sorry. God had never forsaken me, no matter how many times I had relapsed. The perverted behavior when I was high, stuff too embarrassing to write about in this book, He had witnessed all of it.

Filled with shame and remorse, I slowly made my way to the middle row of chairs. Everyone around me was singing, many with their hands in the air. I just stood silently sobbing, arms hanging down at my side, looking straight ahead, tears flowing like an open faucet, dripping off my chin.

Why would God want anything to do with a wretch like me? I don't deserve to be here. I don't deserve another chance. I don't deserve —

"I love you, Scott. I love you, Scott."

God suddenly, audibly, spoke those eight words to me! I had never heard His voice before, nor have I heard it since. My tears continued to flow, but now they were tears of inexpressible joy!

After the service, I ran up to some people I knew and excitedly told them what happened. "God spoke to me! He said 'I love you, Scott. I love you, Scott.'" They just gave me a funny look. That's ok. I didn't bother to explain the significance or the back story. That would take a while, and I just wanted to soak in the reality of God and His relentless love.

I'll be honest, my faith took a giant leap forward that day. Whereas I had always believed God was real in the past, I now knew it for a certainty. And since that day, I have had complete assurance that He is always with me, and that His relentless love for me can never be shaken. It's a wonderful feeling.

Three years later, on almost the exact same date, I listened as Pastor Caesar was delivering a sermon at New Hope International Church. After reading a passage of scripture from the Bible, in which a particular verse was repeated twice, Pastor Caesar then looked out at the congregation and said:

"When God wants you to know something for sure, He says it twice."

39

60th Birthday Gifts

The following weekend was my 60th birthday. Since I would be so close to my dad's when I drove back to New Hope International Church for Sunday service, I took a chance and called him to ask if it would be ok to stop by and say 'Hi.' To my surprise, he said that would be fine.

When I got to my dad's house, I asked him how it felt to have a 60-year-old child. A blank look covered his face, and then it dawned on him that I was referring to myself. We chatted for a few minutes and then I went downstairs to get some clothes and books. When I came back up to leave, he handed me a large brown paper bag. Whatever was in it was heavy. I thanked him and went to church. On the way, I couldn't resist the urge to peek inside the bag - it was my long lost coin collection! I was thrilled! What a great birthday gift from my dad.

At church, my friend Tari also gave me a brown paper bag. Inside were the several sets of sermon CD's she had promised to bring when I saw her the week before. I had informed her then that my truck was having serious issues and that I would have to attend a church closer to where I lived for a while. She told me the CD's were mine to keep, and suggested I listen to the set concerning spiritual warfare first. It was titled "Our Hidden Enemy."

As soon as I got back to Charlie's, I pulled everything out of the bag my dad had given me. When I was 11 and 12 years old, I had worked as a paperboy delivering newspapers. My dad would exchange my earnings at the bank for coin rolls so I could look for old coins, and I had always wondered what had happened to them. Now here they were – coin books filled with mercury dimes, liberty half dollars, buffalo nickels, Indian head pennies and silver quarters. Several rolls of duplicate silver coins were missing, but that was OK with me.

I remember collecting all of them - all except one. It was about the size of a nickel, gold colored and inscribed "1902 $5 Liberty". Weird, where did this coin come from? So I looked it up on the internet and found out that it was pure gold and valued at over $400. Wow! Are you kidding me? Charlie was now charging me rent, and I was short on money because we only worked a day or two each week. So I called a coin shop to see what they would give me for that coin, hoping for half the book value. They said they would pay the full $400! An hour later I had four $100 bills in my hand. I couldn't believe it. This was a gift from heaven.

As wonderful as this sounds, the CDs that Tari gave me would ultimately prove much more valuable. They were all Scripture-based and a virtual treasure trove of spiritual nourishment. During that winter in Silverdale, I listened to them all, and particularly enjoyed the personal testimonies of miraculous healings in the set titled "The Laying on of Hands."

Little did I know then that shortly before heading back to North Dakota in the spring, I would experience a miraculous healing myself.

40

One Step Program

That winter was unusually cold and drizzly, and the surveying assignments were few and far between, which was fine with me. It wasn't the work that bothered me, it was the locations that gave me the fits; driving into or through parts of Seattle where I had been when using crack.

Hearing God's voice had strengthened my resolve to stay clean, no matter what. But that didn't lessen my desire. There is no cure, only ways to cope, and one way of learning to cope was by my attending H.A.D. ministry meetings two nights a week in Silverdale. H.A.D stood for Hope for Addictions/Dependencies, or as we liked to call it, Hope After Dope. It was led by Carrie Ahrendt, who was totally committed to transforming lives through the sharing of Jesus' redemptive grace.

The meetings always started with everyone circling up and singing Christian songs. Then we would recite the seven biblically based principles Carrie used to govern our recovery. Next, anyone who wished to could share with the group whatever was on their mind. Finally, Carrie would close the meetings in prayer. What a wonderful alternative to the secular AA meetings based on the Twelve Steps of Alcoholics Anonymous, where the main focus was on staying clean and sober. Carrie's ministry focused on Jesus.

† † †

On March 23, 2012, I experienced a strong urge to attend a Revival service at New Hope International Church. Even though the service was being held at night 75 miles away, and my truck was not running well at all, I just felt I needed to make the effort to be there. If my truck broke down on the way, so be it. At least God would know I had tried.

By now I had listened to all the CDs Tari had given me, and the set she had recommended, 'Our Hidden Enemies,' had really helped me better understand spiritual warfare. It included several testimonies from people, including the head pastor at New Hope, who had been set free from demonic influences. I was now ready to go on the offensive.

I arrived that evening not knowing what to expect. After singing several songs, we were invited to come forward to be prayed over. This was something I had always been a bit hesitant to join before because watching people fall to the floor was something I still couldn't get used to. I had tried participating a couple of times but would get frustrated when I didn't feel anything, so I would just purposely fall backward.

From the CDs, I had learned that it was quite natural not always to feel an invisible power causing you to fall, but simply surrendering yourself was a nonverbal way of telling God to have His way with you.

As I stood there in the second row, with my eyes closed, I could hear the pastor speaking a word or a short sentence to each person as he got closer to me.

"God, I don't care if I have to come up here a 1000 times, I want to feel something," I prayed silently, and before I knew what happened, I was flat on my back on the floor, with the pastor kneeling beside me. Normally he would have just continued down the line to the next person.

With one hand on my head and the other on my heart, he began speaking with authority: "All generational curses are broken, in Jesus name!" He said more, but that's all I can remember because I started going into convulsions. Then I went completely limp, and a tingling sensation filled my head. The pastor stood up and moved on to the next person in line. I just lay there as my head continued to tingle from ear to ear for several minutes. It was an awesome feeling.

When I finally stood up, I felt woozy and staggered to the back of the church where I saw Pastor Caesar. He was one of the assistant pastors, and I tried to explain to him what I had just experienced, but I couldn't talk very well, and I apologized for slurring my words.

"You're drunk," he said softly.

I knew what he meant. I was drunk - in the Holy Spirit.

"Cool," I said, grinning.

"We've been praying for you," he responded, his eyes welling up with tears.

I stumbled out the door and across the parking area to

my truck. As I was getting in, I looked back and saw what appeared to be an enormous star, almost the size of the sun, low in the sky directly above the church. It looked like something you'd see on a Christmas card, with a long angle of light coming out at the top and bottom, and a shorter angle of light coming out each side. I just stood staring at it for several minutes, not believing what I was witnessing; trying to figure out whether it was real or some sort of a vision. Either way, it was an amazing sight!

It was after 10pm as I drove back through Seattle on my way home to Silverdale. Earlier, on my drive to the Revival, I had been tormented by the usual anxiety attacks that I always experienced in or near the places where I had used. Now they didn't occur at all; I felt complete peace for the first time ever in Seattle. I believe that whatever used to torment me had been expelled when I was convulsing on the floor.

The next morning, a loud rattling sound rang out when I tried to start my truck. So, Charlie gave me a tow to his mechanic's shop. Diagnosis: broken timing belt, plus other miscellaneous problems. The repair estimate came to $840. I didn't care, even though that was going to eat up my entire savings. I just thanked God, knowing He had kept it running just long enough to get me to the Revival.

Charlie and I worked a few more jobs before I realized that even though we continued to travel in and through areas that brought back bad memories of my drug use, these memories no longer ignited within me the usual desire and craving to use. I didn't notice this immediately because it didn't even enter my mind that I should be feeling those temptations. They were foreign to me, or I should say, the NEW me. I was no longer an addict!

I know, they say there is no cure for drug addiction and that recovery lasts a lifetime. Well, of all the miracles chronicled in the Old Testament, no one had ever restored a blind person's sight. That had been unheard of too - until Jesus came along.

A few months later I was watching a segment on the Today Show which featured a man who had suffered a severe head injury and was in a coma for several weeks. When he came out of his coma, he was a virtuoso pianist, even though he had never played a musical instrument in his life. The medical profession said that what had happened to him was a rare phenomenon, known simply as 'a rewiring of the brain.'

God could have rewired my brain without manifesting the tingling sensation I had experienced, but He wanted me to know something supernatural was happening.

AA's 'Twelve Step' programs help a lot of people cope with the struggle of being in recovery. By the grace of God, I went from recovery to RECOVERED.

I call it God's 'One Step' program.

41

On the Road Again

Cured, healed, delivered - set free! I had never dreamed such a miracle could happen, had never even considered the possibility. Addiction - rehab, relapse, rehab, relapse . . . ten horrible years . . . on and on and on and . . . now, just GONE!

The second week of April I drove out to North Dakota to meet up with Charlie. He had gone out earlier to set up camp and had hired a seasoned surveyor to join our crew. We were there three weeks when my eldest son Sean's mom called me from Connecticut to ask if I could come help her sell and move out of her condominium.

It was just the excuse I needed to move on. As much as I appreciated Charlie giving me a job, I wasn't looking forward to living in a trailer in the middle of nowhere, doing work I had no passion for. Charlie said it would be ok for me to take off.

Connecticut ended up being a six-week project, culminating with Sean and his girlfriend Vanessa flying in from Maui to take his mom with them back to Hawaii. I then drove back across the country to spend the summer in Gordon's trailer at Priest Lake.

When Fall rolled around, I drove down to visit my son Kevin in Palm Springs for a few days. While there, my son Bryan's mom asked if I could pick up two flat screen TV's from storage near San Diego and deliver them to Bryan who was now attending college in San Francisco and living on campus. I did, and the 900-mile round trip was worth the few precious minutes I got to spend with my youngest son.

After spending a couple more nights on Kevin's living room couch back in Palm Springs, I decided to head out to Prescott, Arizona. I was getting low on money, so I spent the first few nights sleeping in my truck parked at a Walmart. Eventually, I found a room to rent for $300, and spent every day at an employment agency applying for jobs, with no luck.

Then the family I had met on my first trip to Connecticut invited me to come and live with them in Texas. I figured I might as well give it a try. Two days and 1270 miles later I arrived at their home in Sugar Land, an upscale community located about 25 miles west of Houston. I researched churches, settled on River Pointe Church in Richmond, and immediately began volunteering with their video productions department.

I also started attending one of their home Bible study groups. Usually, the person leading the Bible study would choose a particular chapter to discuss. When it was my turn to lead, I asked if they could give me a month to prepare, and then use the time to share my personal testimony. Everyone said that would be great.

Sharing my story was something that had been on my heart for some time, and this forced me to get it together. With fifteen pages of chronologically organized bullet points, supported by Scripture verses, I bared my soul nonstop for close to two hours. Afterward, I felt a huge sense of relief; there, I had done it. The woman who hosted the Bible study, Ann Gardner, also happened to be the prayer team leader at River Pointe Church. At church the following Sunday, Ann walked up to me and told me that my testimony was very powerful.

In March, the Workmen's Comp issue that had been dragging along for the past couple of years was finally settled, and not a day too soon, as I was flat broke. I gave 10% off the top to charity, $4500 went toward child support owed, and I was able to pay off two personal loans. This left me with about $9500. For the first time in years, I would not have to worry about finances. What a blessing!

My intention when coming to Texas was to stay until spring and then head back up to Priest Lake, and hopefully find work there. I knew that Gordon had sold his trailer, and had no idea where I would live when I got there. But I also knew I would be miserable in the heat and humidity of a Texas summer.

The pastor of New Hope International Church was holding a Revival in San Diego on April 10th, so I timed my departure from Texas to enable me to attend. I drove to my son Kevin's place in Palm Springs, stayed a few days, and went to the Revival. As I made my way from where I had parked my truck to the church, I walked past a guy sitting on the curb lighting a crack pipe. The only emotion I felt was empathy.

After the Revival I went back to Kevin's in Palm Springs for a couple more days, then up to visit Bryan in San Francisco, where I stayed overnight in a hostel. I called the lady friend from high school who had taken me in years earlier at her home near Carnation, Washington, and asked if I could regroup at her house for a couple days before heading over to Priest Lake. She said yes, but two nights was the limit.

Although I was extremely thankful for the amazing ways God continued to provide for me as I bopped around the country, I couldn't help but think of how nice it would be to settle down. Even the Israelites, after roaming in the wilderness, eventually entered the Promised Land. Was there a 'Promised Land' in my future?

I was about to find out.

42

Promised Land

The woman I had called was now living in Tacoma, Washington. The day after my arrival I called a friend in Priest Lake and was given permission to stay at her place while looking for a room to rent. Then I called my dad. I hadn't seen nor spoken with him since my birthday visit in November of 2011.

"Hi dad, it's Scott."

"What do you want?" He responded dryly.

"Well, I just drove from Texas to Tacoma, will be heading to Priest Lake tomorrow, and was wondering if I could stop by and see you on my way out of town."

"That's not a good idea," he replied.

"Why not?" I asked.

"No one in the family wants you around," he stated flatly.

"That's not true. Why do you say that?"

"Your past," he growled.

"Everything is good with the family and me. We had a great time at the lake last year," I pleaded.

Silence. I didn't see any reason to press the issue.

"Well, maybe I can see you in the future sometime," I finally said.

"Goodbye," he said, and hung up.

Ok, at least I had tried. His attitude didn't surprise me, nor was I offended. It might be irritating, but I had accepted him for who he was. My only concern was doing right on my end.

I then decided to check in with my sister Amy. When I told her I was in Tacoma on my way to Priest Lake, she said she and my brother and sisters wanted me to move in with my dad. This was quite a surprise. Apparently, his dementia was getting worse, and he needed constant assistance.

I told Amy I appreciated the invite and said I'd be happy to help out, but that wasn't going to happen based on the conversation I had just had with him. She insisted I stay with her family in Bellevue for a few days to give them time to talk him into it. I expressed my doubts but said I'd come over to their house the next day. She then said that if I did end up going to the lake, they wanted me to stay at our family cabin. Wow! This was great news; I had not been allowed to spend a night there in years.

† † †

A couple of days after arriving at Amy's I attended Sunday service at New Hope International Church. They had moved to a larger facility, and it now just happened to be within walking distance from Amy's house. After the sermon, I lined up to be prayed over. It should be noted that the pastor didn't know of my drug history when he was led to break generational curses at the revival on March 23, 2012. When he stood before me on this day, he didn't know about my homelessness either, but was inspired to speak just two words when he came and stood in front of me: "Promised land."

The next morning I got a call from my sister Shannon.

"Scott, dad just called me, and he's all riled up."

"What's he all riled up about?" I asked.

"He's really shook up about a dream he had last night, and now thinks it would be a good idea if you came and lived with him."

Talk about a 180! It must have been the mother of all dreams. My dad is the last person on earth you would expect to get frightened by anything. Three days later, there I was at my dad's, watching as my niece Mason decorated my room. I would live there for over two years.

I never did ask my dad about the dream he had.

I just thanked God for bringing me out of the wilderness.

43

A Time of Refreshing

This time around I had a completely different mindset about being back at my dad's house. First and foremost, considering how everything had transpired, I had no doubt that God had orchestrated all the events leading up to my living there. I knew I was where God wanted me to be. Secondly, I was also no longer an addict.

Thoughts of using, the restlessness and cravings, no longer existed. I could just settle in and live a normal life. Lastly, I had a purpose for being there – to help my family by caring for our dad. The other times I had lived there, it had always been about my dad taking care of me. Now his dementia had progressed to the point that made it difficult, if not impossible, for him to live alone.

The first thing I noticed after moving in was a bowl filled with the Father's Day and Christmas cards I had sent every year while I was away. I had never gotten a response from him, so seeing them opened and saved was a pleasant surprise.

One day my dad showed me a baseball autographed by his Gonzaga teammates and asked if I knew what it was. I did; it was from a perfect game he had pitched in college against the University of Montana. I told my dad I remembered getting into a little hot water for the scratches on it. He fell silent for a moment, and then said something I never thought I'd hear.

"I'm sorry for some of the things I did."

Oh my goodness, I was so happy to hear him say that, and I realized he had been living with a sense of guilt all these years. I told him thanks, not to worry about it, and that I was sorry about many things I had done as well.

My sister Amy and her husband Keith asked if I would help out with their daughter Mason who was in 5th grade. I said absolutely! So three days a week I would drive Mason home from school and tutor her in math, staying with her until her dad got home from work. At my dad's I kept busy cleaning the house, doing yard work and walking the dog. I also got into playing a lot of pickleball at the Community Center – three times a week for up to four hours each session. It was a lot of fun and great exercise.

The only negative issue I had to deal with was an ongoing dispute with the California Child Support agency. Long story short, they claimed I owed $4000, refusing to acknowledge the fact that I had paid that money through Hawaii Child support. When I finally started receiving social security, they swooped in and took half my monthly check. I was devastated.

At church the Sunday after this happened, the pastor asked for donations above and beyond our regular tithes to help fund a mission trip to Thailand. My first thought was: I had only brought money for my tithe into the church, so I won't be giving any extra. My second thought was that morning I had put $40 in the glove compartment of my truck. I felt God testing me, considering what had just started happening with my social security checks. I retrieved the $40 and anonymously donated it.

The next morning, while out walking the dog, my cell phone rang. It was the California Child Support agency calling to let me know that they now agreed with the fact that I did not owe them anything.

Are you kidding me?! I had gotten nowhere with them over a period of two years of letters and phone calls, and now, when all hope was lost; suddenly, a change of heart? I knew that this must be the outcome of faithfully sowing the $40 into the Missions trip and trusting God, no matter what. God is no man's debtor. They apologized, said they would refund what was taken, and rescind the garnish they had placed on my social security. I was overjoyed!

† † †

In the summer of 2014 my dad's dementia had progressed to where he was no longer able to drive. The Department of Motor Vehicles took his license away and he wasn't the least bit happy about it, but graciously signed his car over to me. I then sold my truck for $600.

Dad's condition continued to worsen over the next few months and eventually reached the point where I was no longer able to care for him. The family decided we needed to move him into assisted living. We had tried a couple of times before, but my dad refused each time because he said I was caring for him. I took my siblings' advice to go on a month long road trip in February of 2015, and they were able to move him while I was away.

I drove south, visiting my dad's sister in Northern California, my sons Bryan and Kevin in Southern California, and over to Texas to retrieve stuff I had left there in 2013 (when I thought I'd be right back after a summer at Priest Lake. Praise be to God, a dream had changed that scenario.)

44

Coins and Dental Blessing

By the time I returned from my trip, my dad had been settled into an assisted living facility. I spent the next three months landscaping and clearing everything out of the house so that it could be sold. When I was done, my brother came by to check on things, and I showed him the only item that was left in the house - an old safe in the basement that was too heavy to move.

He told me just to leave it, and asked if I had checked to see if there was anything inside. I said I had, and that it was empty. He looked inside and noticed a small wooden door, about four inches square, and asked if I had opened it. I told him it was locked and I wasn't able to find a key that fit. My brother said we should check anyway, just in case there was anything valuable inside.

So I took a hammer, busted out the little door and, lo and behold, wedged inside were the rolls of duplicate silver coins that had been missing from my coin collection. They were worth over $1500! I was ecstatic!

Shortly after discovering the coins, I experienced another totally unexpected blessing. The people I played pickleball with at the Community Center had been bugging me for quite some time to go to the University of Washington Dental School and get an estimate of how much it would cost to fix my teeth. As you can imagine, they were in terrible shape from all the years I was an addict. I kept telling them I'd go, but procrastinated and never got around to it.

When my dad's house sold, I told them I'd be leaving soon, and that's when they let me in on the reason for their interest in getting my teeth checked out. Behind my back, they had taken up a collection to help with the expense, and over 30 people had given donations. I was so overwhelmed with gratitude I immediately made the appointment.

The initial estimate came in at $2400, which was a really good price. I didn't know how much the people at the community center had collected but figured whatever it was I'd make up the difference. When I told them the price, they said they had it covered - and that was when I learned they had collected nearly $3000! I hardly knew these people, had only met them when playing pickleball, and yet they were moved to raise this money on my behalf. I started crying.

At my second dental appointment, other issues were discovered and the price went up to $4400. I told the donors that I would just have some but not all of the dental procedures done to keep the cost near the original estimate. However, they insisted I do it right, and raised an additional

$1400! I will forever be grateful to these amazing, kind-hearted folks for their incredible generosity.

Dental appointments were scheduled for the next six weeks, and I was able to find temporary housing at a ministry near Seattle run by someone I had met during my days at the Cross Discipleship. In mid-September, after my last dental procedure, the dental school informed me that it would take several months for my mouth to heal before they could continue and finish the work. The family I had lived with in Texas suggested I come back in the meantime and stay with them. That sounded good to me. I missed volunteering with the media department at River Pointe Church. Plus, I could visit my sons Bryan and Kevin in Southern California on the way to Texas and on the way back.

I had one other purpose in mind when I got to Texas, something that had been on my heart and would eventually take four years to accomplish: sharing my testimony by writing a book.

45

Texas, Idaho, Texas, MAUI

Over the next few months down in Texas I managed to complete about half of the rough draft on my book project and volunteered with the video crews every weekend at River Pointe Church. In mid-April, I made the drive back to Seattle to finish the dental work, visiting my sons Bryan and Kevin, and my dad's sister in California along the way.

A friend who lived near my dad's old house told me I could stay at a second home she owned, but on the day she was to give me the key, she changed her mind. I then found a room on craigslist, but on the day I was to move in, the owners said they rented it to someone else.

These setbacks convinced me that God had a better plan, although I had no idea what it was. I decided to go to our family cabin in Priest Lake, Idaho, even though this meant I would have to drive 350 miles each way once a week for the next four weeks to my dental appointments.

A couple of days after arriving at the lake, I went to visit my elderly friend Lucy on the other side of the lake only to find she had passed away during the winter. The people staying at her house were surprised no one had told me, and after sharing Lucy stories with them, I went to a nearby store to get a newspaper. As I drove away, I noticed the store had a 'Help Wanted' sign on the door. I kept driving, all the while battling a feeling that I should find out what the job was. Ten miles later I gave in, turned around, went back to the store, and I got an application.

The next morning I turned in the completed application, and a week later the owner called to ask if I could come in for an interview. When we met, after talking for just a few minutes, he said something was telling him that I would work out just fine. I was hired and worked at the store until business dropped off when the summer tourist season ended in early September.

Back down to Texas I went, making the usual stops along the way. This time I rented a room off Craigslist and hoped to finish the rough draft of my book project. It felt so good to reunite with the media teams at River Pointe Church. It's hard to describe how wonderful I feel being there, utilizing the skills God has given me to serve Him.

I didn't know where I would be going in the spring, but I did know I wanted to be on Maui for Sean's wedding in July. Out of curiosity, I searched the internet to see how Haggai Institute (the ministry I had done some video work for back when I had my productions company on Maui) was doing. I discovered they had volunteer opportunities that provided airfare, room, and board. So I called them about applying as a volunteer grounds keeper, and they emailed me an application packet which required three letters of reference – one from my pastor, one from someone who knew me well, and one from my most recent employer. Thank the Lord I had gotten that summer job at the lake! The owner of the store wrote a wonderful reference letter, as did the pastor at River Pointe who oversees the media department, and the prayer team leader who had heard my testimony.

Sean, Vanessa, and my two-year-old grandson lived less than two miles from Haggai Institute, so if I got accepted as a volunteer, I could visit them on a regular basis. They were expecting their second child in March, and the wedding date was set for July 22nd. I mailed my application on December 2nd, and on Christmas Day 2016, I received an email from Haggai Institute notifying me that I had been accepted. They scheduled me from April 11th through August 31st.

I was going back to Maui.

46

Blessed

Sean asked if I could stay with them for a week before checking in at Haggai to help Vanessa care for the children, so I flew in a week before my volunteering would begin. He lived in Kihei, and it had changed little since I had left fourteen years earlier. I had changed a lot, thank God. No longer self-centered, worrying and concerned primarily with my own interests, I was now Christ-centered, appreciative of the opportunity to live, serve and fellowship with like-minded women and men who knew and loved God.

Sean met me at the airport, and thirty minutes later I was holding my newest grandson, Amari Kamrin Curran, just two weeks old. My other grandson, Kawhi Mykel, kept his distance, curious about this stranger. It had been almost two years since Sean and Vanessa had visited the Mainland to celebrate his first birthday, so his behavior was expected. Thankfully, as I regularly visited during the next few months, Kawhi slowly warmed up to “Papa” Scott.

On April 11th I checked into Haggai Institute. When I had applied, I requested grounds keeping, but also told the volunteer coordinator I would do anything, even clean toilets. Sure enough, that's what I did my first two weeks - clean toilets. Then I was moved to the grounds keeping crew.

There were about 25 volunteers when I arrived, all from the US and Canada. It was great getting to know them and to share our testimonies. Throughout my almost five-month stay, other volunteers would complete their commitment and be replaced by new volunteers, some from as far away as Australia and Hamburg, Germany. They were all amazing, wonderful people, totally committed to serving the Lord. Over half of them were returning volunteers, some having come back regularly for several years.

Then there were the participants - what an inspiration they were! During my stay, I met Christian men and women from over 40 countries; Russia, China, India, Pakistan, Egypt, Ethiopia, Kenya, Malaysia, Vietnam, Peru and Honduras, just to name a few. Some were involved in full-time ministry, but most were business owners, doctors, college professors, judges, politicians, government officials, etc. All were highly successful in their chosen fields, and all shared one thing in common - a fervent love for Jesus and a burning desire to learn how to effectively share their faith in their home nations.

To experience God moving in and through these Christians from around the world, transforming lives and bringing hope to the hopeless, was an incredible blessing. It reinforced my own commitment to redeem the time I have remaining on this earth to serve God and proclaim the good news of salvation through faith in Jesus, our Lord and Savior.

My volunteer schedule allowed me to spend some evenings and almost every weekend with my grandsons. This helped Sean and Vanessa, and enabled me to develop a relationship with my grandsons who would have rarely seen me if Haggai hadn't approved my application. I was doubly blessed!

Bryan and Kevin came to Maui for a few days in July for Sean and Vanessa's wedding. It was the second time that year (the other time was my dad's memorial service in Seattle in January) that all my sons were together again. In almost twenty years, 2017 was the first year I was blessed to have all three of my sons together on two different occasions in the same year.

† † †

My volunteering ended on August 27th, and I was scheduled to fly back to the Mainland soon after. As the day approached, Sean asked if I could stay a while longer at their home before leaving Maui. He wanted to go with friends on a hunting trip to Montana for ten days in mid-September, and Vanessa could use my help with the kids while he was gone. I said absolutely, anything to help out. So, we rescheduled my departure flight to September 28th, and I moved into his home after my last day at Haggai International on August 31st.

What happened next was something neither Sean, nor I could have ever imagined. I can only thank God that I could be at my son's side when he needed me the most.

47

"I'm scared, dad"

Sean had a fever of 103 degrees when I arrived at his home. This was unusual because he rarely ever got sick. The next day his temperature was still high, so he asked me to drive him to the clinic where they took blood and urine samples. The doctor said it would be several days before the results came back from the lab, therefore he prescribed some antibiotics for Sean and sent us on our way.

A couple of days later the clinic called and informed us that we needed to take Sean immediately to the Emergency Room. Although they didn't have a definite diagnosis, they suspected kidney and/or liver problems based on the analysis of Sean's urine sample. By now Sean had begun experiencing excruciating pain in his abdomen, so Vanessa drove him to the hospital on the other side of the island while I stayed at home with the kids. Later that evening she called to let me know that another set of blood samples and tests revealed Sean's white blood cell count was low. There was no definitive diagnosis of what the problem was as yet, but they would be staying overnight in the hospital, and more blood draws would be taken and analyzed in the morning.

I immediately put the word out to my Christian brothers and sisters at Haggai International and on the Mainland, to please pray for my son. The response was overwhelming. In the meantime, Sean's condition continued to deteriorate over the next couple of days. Vanessa's mom eventually came over to watch the kids, so I could visit my son at the hospital.

I was wearing my 'Jesus' hat when I walked into the hospital lobby. When the receptionist remarked that she liked my hat, I knew right away she was Christian, and I shared with her the reason I was at the hospital. I then went up to Sean's room and stood at the foot of his bed while Vanessa sat next to him. He was obviously in a lot of pain, grimacing and clutching his abdomen with both hands.

"I'm scared, dad," Sean said as he looked up at me.

"You're going to be ok Sean," I responded confidently. "I guarantee it. I'm not just saying this. You're going to be ok."

My statement was full of faith, and I truly believed it. I was giving him the only encouraging news since he became ill. Everything else had been negative; including the results of numerous blood draws that had been taken since he arrived. His insides were imploding, his white blood cell count was continuing to drop, and the doctor had no idea why. There was no way to know what treatment should be prescribed.

As much as I was concerned about my son's health, I was equally, if not more, concerned about the state of my son's soul. God tells us that whoever asks Jesus to be their Lord and Savior will never die but have eternal life. Sean had never asked for that life. I felt so sad and sorry for my son, knowing he was facing his eternal destiny with fear and uncertainty. I excused myself and went down to the lobby to ask the receptionist if she knew of any hospital chaplains. She said she knew a Pastor Dan who regularly visited patients. I asked her to call him to visit with my son. Although I had never been able to interest Sean in Christianity, I knew my son would definitely acknowledge how my faith had changed my life.

She called Pastor Dan, and he said he would come over to visit with Sean in the evening.

I thanked her, got her cell phone number, then went back to my son's room to ask if he would be ok with Pastor Dan's visit, and he was. The next morning I called Vanessa and asked if the Pastor had shown up. She said that he had, that he was very friendly and had shared some stories and then prayed for Sean. Ok, I thought, at least this was a start.

Vanessa continued to keep me updated on Sean's condition. His kidneys, liver, and gallbladder were continuing to deteriorate. Then one morning she called to inform me that Sean had been moved to the Intensive Care Unit. The hospital was preparing to medivac him to a larger hospital on the island of Oahu as his white blood cell count had plummeted and was now critically low. A team of doctors would be waiting when he arrived, including a transplant specialist.

Instantly, I became overwhelmingly burdened for my son's salvation. In layman's terms, I completely freaked out! In desperation, I called the woman I had met at the hospital; sobbing, I told her what was happening, and that she had to get Pastor Dan to lead my son to Christ NOW. She said she would call him right away.

Thankfully, Vanessa's mom was with me at the house helping with the kids. We were short on baby formula, so I went to the store to buy some before driving across the island, hopefully in time to see Sean before the ambulance took him to the airport. As I walked out of the store, I saw the pastor of Hope Chapel (the church I was attending while on Maui). Breaking down again, I quickly told him what was going on with my son. I asked him if he could have a pastor from Hope Chapel go to the hospital in case Pastor Dan didn't make it. He immediately got on his cell phone and left a message with Kaitee Lusk who headed the church's hospital ministry team.

Then, he said a prayer with me, that God would heal my son, and most importantly, cause my son to put his faith in Jesus.

48

"It's all good!"

After dropping off the baby supplies at the house, I raced to the hospital. Walking into Sean's room, I asked Vanessa if a pastor had come by that morning. When she answered in the affirmative, I walked over and leaned next to Sean's head.

"Did you ask Jesus to come into your heart?" I quietly asked.

"Yes, I did," Sean responded.

Filled with an incredible sense of relief, I stepped back, spread my arms out wide, and with a big smile proclaimed: "It's all good!"

Just then, a man about my son's age entered the room.

"Hi, I'm Pastor Dan."

"Thank you so much for coming by earlier," I said as I shook his hand.

"I didn't come by earlier" he responded.

Come to find out, this was another Pastor Dan. He, and

others from his church, King's Cathedral, had been told about my prayer request for my son when they had gone to Haggai International to pray for the ministry. Unbeknownst to me, he had also been praying for my son all this time, and had now come to the hospital to visit him in the Intensive Care Unit.

I thanked him for coming and asked him to say a prayer. We all laid hands on Sean as Pastor Dan prayed. Just as he finished the EMT's arrived. They put Sean on a gurney and wheeled him to the ambulance for the ride to the airport. He and Vanessa were then medivaced to the hospital on Oahu.

Despite all that was happening, I was filled with an incredible sense of calm assurance as I drove back to the house. I thanked God for lots of things during that car ride, but notably for all the people praying for my son, and for both Pastor Dans. What can I say? I was just really happy!

Vanessa called that evening and said the hospital had been amazed that Sean wasn't in a coma when he arrived, based on the reports they had received. Several specialists had done more tests and would be determining a treatment plan based upon the results the next morning.

The next day all the tests came back negative, meaning they still could not come up with a diagnosis as to what was causing his organs to deteriorate. The source of his illness was a complete mystery, and his condition continued to worsen, as it had been doing every day since he first started feeling sick. His liver and kidneys were failing, and his temperature continued to spike near 103 degrees. That evening the doctors announced they planned to put him on dialysis the next day in anticipation for the need of a liver and kidney transplant.

God had other plans.

In the morning, Sean's condition hadn't gotten any better, but it hadn't gotten any worse either! His white blood cell count had been dropping every day, but on this day it remained where it had been the day before; extremely low, but not lower. The doctors couldn't explain why it hadn't continued to worsen, so they postponed dialysis for a day in the hope that whatever was causing the illness might have crested.

Sure enough, to everyone's amazement, the next day Sean's white blood cell count was on the rebound, and his temperature was almost normal. He continued to improve from that point on, and after several more days in the hospital, he was well enough to return home.

Sean had been there for me years earlier during my darkest days, and now God had given me the opportunity to be there for him. This was such a remarkable turn of events it could only have been orchestrated by God.

What an awesome God we serve!

Epilogue

Sean's condition continued to improve, and though his kidneys are operating at 50% of normal, the doctors say that this is sufficient for him to live a normal life. Within a couple of months, he was back to working, hunting, fishing and playing softball. Praise God!

I left Maui two weeks after Sean got out of the hospital, stayed in Seattle for two nights, then drove south to my Aunt Cherie's place in northern California for several days of rest and relaxation. My next stop was Palm Springs for a few days to visit with my son Kevin, and from there back to Texas. I kept busy for the next six months volunteering again with the video production teams at River Pointe Church and continuing to work on writing this book.

It was during this time that I read "The Master's Call," the true story of four Muslim people who converted to Christianity. It is an amazing testimony, beautifully written by Anna D'Souza. I contacted Anna and asked if she would be willing to help with the writing of my testimony. She graciously accepted, I was thrilled, and you, the reader, are reaping the benefits of Anna's gifted and enjoyable writing skills.

In the spring of 2018 I drove back to visit with Kevin for a few days in Palm Springs, and then flew from there to Maui and spent a month with Sean's family before beginning a three-month summer stint volunteering again at Haggai

International. What an incredible blessing it is to be able to see my grandsons and serve the Lord at the same time. My son Bryan came for a visit when I returned to Kevin's in September. And then I made the drive back to Texas and River Pointe Church.

God willing, I plan to continue serving with the media team at River Pointe Church every fall thru spring and at Haggai International during the summers, redeeming the time God has given me for His glory. There is no higher calling than serving the Lord, it is my only desire, and I am truly grateful to God for His relentless love that has made all of this possible.

Reflections and Encouragement

"Pistol" Pete Maravich, the flamboyant basketball player, was my favorite athlete while growing up. I wanted what Pete had: amazing basketball skills, the adoration of the crowd, fame, and fortune. I couldn't imagine a better life. It wasn't until a few years ago, after reading Mark Kriegel's excellent biography titled "Pistol," that I discovered that Pete Maravich was sad, confused and miserable. Nothing he tried, which was just about everything, including alcohol, Hinduism and belief in extraterrestrials, gave Pete lasting relief from the emptiness he felt deep in his soul. His search for true and permanent happiness continued throughout his playing days, and into retirement.

Then early one morning, after a sleepless and restless night, he turned to God and cried out for forgiveness, and God responded in an audible voice: "Be strong and lift thine own heart."

The impact on Pete was immediate and permanent. He dove headfirst into his new found Christian faith, reading and studying the Bible daily. He preached and shared his testimony wherever and whenever possible, and with the same exuberance and dedication he had applied to basketball. Joy filled the emptiness in his soul; he had finally found peace in the Prince of Peace - Jesus Christ.

It is interesting to note that Pete Maravich should never

have survived playing basketball in the first place. While playing a friendly game with fellow evangelists one day, he suffered a massive heart attack and died. The coroner's report stated that he had been born with only one of the two artery systems that supply blood to the heart. According to cardiologists, this condition is usually fatal before the age of 20, and should have prevented Pete Maravich from participating in any strenuous activity, not the least of which was professional basketball. Pete Maravich was forty years old when he died.

When I reflect on this miracle in Pete's life, as well as the many times I should have died myself before accepting Jesus as my Savior, this Bible verse comes to mind:

I will pardon those whom I preserve.

Jeremiah 50:20[b] NKJV

God sees the end from the beginning. He knew that Pete Maravich and I would eventually ask Jesus to be our Lord and Savior, and He preserved our lives so that He could pardon us when that happened. Our life journeys differed greatly. Pete had worldly pleasures in abundance, and yet was forever searching for what would truly make him happy. I wasn't searching, and needed to be allowed to self-destruct and hit bottom.

And we know that all things work together for good to those who love God, to those who are called according to His purpose.

Romans 8:28 NIV

Certainly, not all things in themselves are good. Being addicted to drugs is not a good thing. But God will use whatever means are necessary, including our horrible decisions and behavior, to cause us to ultimately seek Him and share our testimony of His relentless love with a lost and hurting world.

Therefore, if anyone is in Christ, the new creation has come: the old has gone, the new is here! All this is from God, who reconciled us to himself through Christ and gave us the ministry of reconciliation; that God was reconciling the world to himself in Christ . . . We are therefore Christ's ambassadors, as though God were making His appeal through us.

2 Corinthians 5:17-19[a], 20 NIV

Jesus was struck with a fist, spat upon, ridiculed, whipped by a Roman soldier, had a crown of thorns pressed into His head, and hung for six hours nailed to a cross and died. Jesus, Who had no sin, willingly suffered being tortured and killed, so that the sin debt for all who believe in Him was paid in full.

. . . the Son of Man [Jesus] did not come to be served, but to serve, and to give His life as a Ransom for many.

Mark 10:45 NKJV

Looking unto Jesus . . . Who for the joy set before Him endured the cross, despising its shame . . ..

Hebrews 12:2 NKJV

The 'joy' that enabled Jesus to endure His suffering was in knowing that His sacrifice would make it possible for us to have a personal relationship with Him, not only in this life, but also forever in Heaven.

Jesus stands knocking at the door of your heart, waiting to be invited in. Don't worry about cleaning up the mess inside first. Just open the door. He knows all about the mess anyway, and He's not going to quit knocking; He's not going to walk away. He's also not going to invite Himself in - That's a choice you have to make.

I want to encourage you to read the Bible, find a good church, and pray often. Abundant life in Christ has nothing to do with worldly goods and pleasures; it's all about love, joy, peace, purpose, and an assurance of knowing that God is real, and He loves you.

The relentless love of God saved a wretch like me.

Acknowledgements

To Father God: Thank you for prompting me to share my testimony, and for Your divine inspiration whenever I got stuck, which was more often than not.

To Anna D'Souza: With a family to care for and all your many mission trips around the world, I have no idea how you found the time to collaborate with me on this project. You have an amazing talent for writing, and the revisions you made throughout the manuscript greatly enhanced the final product. Thank you so much, Anna.

To Tari Stotesbery and Ida Smith: No good work is accomplished without a firm foundation built on daily prayer, and I entrusted my two favorite prayer warriors with this mission. Tari and Ida, thank you for your faithfulness. I love you both.

To Haggai International Volunteers: After lending out a copy of my first rough draft to a volunteer friend, word got out and the requests came pouring in. The response was one hundred percent positive, which was very encouraging. Thank you all for your support!

To Keith Brehm and Kara Moats: When I first began writing, Keith, you were my constant source of encouragement and motivation. And Kara, thank you so much for proofreading the final draft.

To Michael Cartwright: Thank you, Michael, for designing the book's cover.

To the countless others: Thank you for inquiring on how the writing was progressing, praying, offering suggestions and sharing your excitement about the project. My heartfelt thanks goes out to you all.

Note from the Author

Dear Reader,

If you wish to contact me, please send an email to: rscottcurran@gmail.com.

I look forward to hearing from you.

Thank you!

Scott Curran

My sons - (from left to right) Bryan, Kevin, Sean at the Family Cabin. Priest Lake, Idaho - August 2011

My son Kevin. Palm Springs, CA - April 2013

Bryan at college. San Francisco, CA - April 2013

Arriving with my dad at his 85th birthday celebration.
Bellevue, WA - July 13, 2013

Sons Kevin and Sean. Priest Lake, Idaho - August 8, 2013

My dear friend Ida Smith at New Hope International Church. Bellevue, WA - June 2014

My brother Mike, his son Brady and my dad.
Seattle, WA - December 26, 2014

Sean, Vanessa and one-year old Kawhi at family cabin.
Priest Lake, Idaho - August 4, 2015

Family cabin's dock. Priest Lake, Idaho

Photo op between games of pickleball.
Stafford, Texas. - October 26, 2015

My son Kevin. Palm Springs, CA - March 30, 2016

My son Bryan. Oceanside, CA - April 1, 2016

The day I sold the 1989 Toyota truck, my transportation and, at times, my home during my travels around the country. Seattle - June 16, 2016

Breakfast with sons Bryan, Kevin and Sean the morning of my dad's memorial service. Seattle - January 28, 2017

Sons Kevin, Bryan & Sean at my dad's memorial service.
Seattle - January 28, 2017

Kevin, Sean, Bryan and Kawhi
at Sean and Vanessa's Wedding. Maui - July 22, 2017

Grandsons 3 yr old Kawhi and 5 month old Amari. Maui - August 20, 2017

Volunteering at Haggai International.
Maui - August 29, 2017

Volunteering at River Pointe Church.
Richmond, Texas - November 26, 2017

Vanessa and Sean leaving their home for a walk with the kids. Maui - May 31, 2018

With Sean at his softball game. Maui - June 2018

Grandsons Kawhi
and Amari.
Maui - June 16, 2018

With volunteer friends in the lobby of Haggai International. Maui - August 15, 2018

Volunteering with Sandra Eilers at Haggai International dinner event. Maui - August 30, 2018

River Pointe Church. Richmond, Texas - April 13, 2019

Volunteering with the media team at River Pointe Church.
Richmond, Texas - April 27, 2019

To God be the Glory!

Made in the USA
Coppell, TX
08 January 2020